# MARRIAGE
## UNDER COVER

*Thriving in a Culture of
Quiet Desperation*

# MARRIAGE
## UNDER COVER

*Thriving in a Culture of
Quiet Desperation*

by Bob and Audrey Meisner
with Stephen W. Nance

**Marriage Under Cover: Thriving in a Culture of Quiet Desperation**

ISBN 0-924748-45-1
UPC 88571300015-4

© 2005 by Bob and Audrey Meisner
Printed in the United States of America

Bob and Audrey Meisner
1111 Chevrier Blvd.
Winnipeg, MB  Canada  R3T 1Y2
(204) 949-3333
www.BobandAudrey.com

Milestones International Publishers
4410 University Drive, Ste. 113
Huntsville, AL  35816
(256) 536-9402, ext. 234; Fax: (256) 536-4530
www.milestonesinternationalpublishers.com

1 2 3 4 5 6 7 8 9 10 11 / 09 08 07 06 05

# Dedication

Dedicated to you, the reader.
There are no coincidences in this life,
and it is by divine appointment that you hold this book.

# Acknowledgments

This book is the part of our journey that has taken us from a place of likely devastation through the curtain of heaven into God's inner sanctuary. When you read it, may you take new courage as you flee to Him, your place of refuge, where you hold to His promise with confidence.

We couldn't have completed this project without the passion and talents of many devoted friends and coworkers.

Within this story are principles of truth that have come alive to us and have been applied directly to our journey of healing. Jim Richards has taught us so much about Who really defines us, and Craig Hill has brought clarity and pertinence to the term *covenant*. Leo and Molly Godzich were the main tools of rescue when adultery threatened to kill our marriage. Ron and Cathy Hembree sacrificed to keep our family together. Lois and T.C. Burkett loved us unconditionally as their own, and Doug Weiss gave us tools in intimacy that we will use forever. Don and Mary Colbert heard the Lord's voice in ministering to our grief and bitterness, and Henry and Donna Wright helped us understand the "why" in what happened. Pastor Tommy Barnett preached to us to love again, and we'll always be grateful to him for giving us a church family that we can call "home."

We've gleaned from the expertise of Gary Chapman when it comes to relationships, and we've never met anyone quite as amazing at talking grace as our dear friend Steve McVey. Don Nori is our friend who understands covering, who always remembers mercy.

Our close friends Steve and Pam held up our arms in battle when we were too weak. Shawna and Gary took us in and gave us love and deep friendship. Lenny and Mariam generously gave and gave, and Arnold and Gwen, Cindy and Tommy, Kim and Randy have been true friends. Gerry and Jan, Pat and Stephanie, and Jeff and Leah accepted us back without any questions and offered friendship through painful times.

Jim Rill and Steve Nance made this book happen. We're thankful for their professional know-how and passion for the message.

Every brother, sister, aunt, uncle, and grandparent on both sides of our family have been extremely supportive and understanding through a time when they could have been resentful and closed. Our thanks go especially to our parents. They gave up every right of their own to give unconditional love to us. They have given generously in every way they could to see us healed, strong, and whole.

Christopher, Janelle, David, and Robert...these Meisner family members are full of life, laughter, and happy memories

## Acknowledgments

because each one has chosen to forgive and embrace faith and supernatural love. Our children have now seen pain, but have experienced the redeeming power of God. Thank you.

The family of God has prayed for us. *It's A New Day* viewers have written letters of encouragement and prayed for us more than we'll ever know. We couldn't have written this book or experienced God's mighty power without the prayers of countless friends and family.

Thank You, Jesus, for the honor of speaking to others about how You bring Your hope when life is seemingly impossible. This book belongs to You, and our prayer is that You will touch the hearts of those who read it, like only You can.

*"The one who calls you is faithful and he will do it"* (1 Thessalonians 5:24, NIV).

# *Endorsements*

Bob and Audrey's incredible story of grace, healing, and victory in the face of adultery is a much-needed corrective to the corrosive influences of a cynical and desperate culture that is increasingly hostile to traditional values, including marriage. *Marriage Under Cover* will by turns sadden you and thrill you, make you laugh and make you cry and ultimately lift you to new heights of understanding God's power to redeem, rescue, and restore.

*Bunny Wilson*
*Speaker, teacher, counselor*
*Best-selling author of* Knight in Shining Armor

Bob and Audrey Meisner's story...is more than testimony, it is a case study in the never-ending and unfailing mercies of God when one chooses to draw near to Him...They evidence the glory of God that exhibits beauty from ashes.

*Tommy Barnett*
*Pastor, Phoenix First Assembly of God*

*Marriage Under Cover* is a story of God's grace and redemption. I highly recommend it.

Gary D. Chapman, Ph.D.
*Best-selling author of* The Five Love Languages

Bob and Audrey Meisner have a remarkable gift for communicating the healing power of God for restoring marriages. This book...is a must-read for all couples who find their union in turmoil or for those who want to prevent marital discord.

Don Colbert, M.D.
*Best-selling author of* What Would Jesus Eat,
Deadly Emotions, Toxic Relief,
*and* The Bible Cure Series

*Marriage Under Cover* will provide hope to struggling couples and provide the necessary tools to help them rebuild their marriage and re-ignite their love for each other.

Mary Colbert
*Author of* Healing for the Wounded Heart

*Marriage Under Cover* will give you hope. It will take you beyond the limitations of this loveless society and superficial spirituality to a Jesus that is real, a gospel that works, and a love that conquers all!

Dr. James B. Richards
*Author of* We Still Kiss

This story of courage, passion, and love is a must-read for every believer. The lesson portrayed in *Marriage Under Cover* is critical for everyone's "happily ever after."

Dr. Doug Weiss, Ph.D., LPC
*Executive Director of Heart to Heart Counseling Center*
*Colorado Springs, CO*

*Endorsements*

This courageous story...is a must-read for every couple concerned about protecting their marriage in these challenging times.

*Ken Gaub*
*Ken Gaub Worldwide Ministries*

Four years ago, when I found out what Audrey did, I thought her life, marriage, and ministry were lost forever. Every day I clung to Job 19:25: *"I know that my Redeemer lives..."* and cried and prayed for a miracle. This book will bring hope to parents who find themselves in a similar predicament.

*Betty Thiessen*
*Founder of* It's A New Day
*Canadian Television*

Bob and Audrey Meisner are tremendous examples of how God's grace is big enough to absorb anything in our lives. *Marriage Under Cover*...will stir your heart and cause you once again to thank God for His amazing grace.

*Dr. Steve McVey*
*Author of* Grace Walk

Audrey and Bob Meisner...laughter after tears...joy through the storm...consistent praise and faithful receiving...life and more life...and a love story that few in this world could ever live or write. Once you read their story...the climate of your life will be changed forever. Read, listen, and *experience!*

*Pam Thum*
*Gospel singer/Songwriter*

Poetry in motion! Bob and Audrey's story will take you through the darkest shadows into the brilliant light of God's grace. Here's proof that true love is possible with God!

*Stephen Marshall*
*Singer/Songwriter/Author*

It has been my joy to love and walk alongside Bob, Audrey, and their family as they worked through "insurmountable" obstacles to find again health and wholeness in their marriage and ministries. They are an absolute treasure to the body of Christ. They show us that "the way back" *is* possible— *redeemingly so!*

*Lois E. Burkett, D.D., D.M.*

Highly recommended! Bob and Audrey...are incredibly transparent, sharing their darkest hours of pain and their path towards a bright future. Their poignant story shows that God is not only a Redeemer, but also a *re-dreamer.*

*Dr. David Hawkins*
*Psychologist and Author of*
When Pleasing Others is Hurting You
*and* Saying It So He'll Listen

Their story will bring hope to your heart.

*Willard Thiessen (Audrey's father)*
*Founder and President of Trinity Television Inc.*
*Host of* It's A New Day

This is a book that demonstrates the boundless mercies of God. It shows forgiveness so complete that a terrible experience actually catapults those involved into a deeper relationship with God, a deeper love for each other, and a more fruitful ministry.

*Don Nori, Sr.*
*CEO of Destiny Image, USA*

## Endorsements

This book honestly confronts all the issues [of adultery]. If this book is read and absorbed, people will get informed on how to overcome these very understandable temptations.

*Kate Wiedrick*

This book is a grand slam! It will shock you with its transparency, transform you with its truth, and help you recapture the wonder of a vibrant relationship with your spouse.

*Phil Callaway*
*Speaker and best-selling author of*
Making Life Rich Without Any Money

Read but don't judge. Read and identify with Bob and Audrey...and learn from their hard lessons and humility.

*Dr. Paul Hawkins*
*Youth With A Mission*

The perfect marriage, marred and nearly destroyed by deception, betrayal, and adultery, but then restored by God's amazing grace. [Bob and Audrey Meisner's] testimony is that the same potent medicine that healed their marriage can now do the same for yours!

*Dennis Weidrick*
*Author and Founder of Weidrick and*
*Associates Apostolic Ministries*

*Marriage Under Cover* addresses a topic the church seldom touches: how to navigate through the murky waters of adultery to restitution. This book...clearly brings home the message that there is hope and healing at the end of our mistakes.

*Michelle McKinney Hammond*
*Author of* The Power of Being a Woman

Bob and Audrey have dedicated themselves to communicating to couples that no mistake, tragedy, sin, or adultery can deter God from accomplishing His purposes in marriage. This book is not just for those whose marriages might be troubled or in crisis, but for every couple seeking true intimacy, fulfillment, and purpose in marriage.

*Craig Hill*
*Founder of Family Foundations International*

Bob and Audrey's journey as "pilgrims in progress" will encourage and help you to recognize similar areas of your own lives. Their open and honest discussion will give the reader compassion for others who are struggling to understand their spiritual and emotional battles.

*Henry W. Wright*
*Pastor and author of* A More Excellent Way

# Contents

# Foreword

✻❧✻

Marriage is under attack today in a greater way than ever before. In addition to the age-old battle of human selfishness and pride that flies in the face of marriage, cultural pressures, visual seductions, and a plethora of relationship issues are hard at work to destroy marriage as we know it. Add to that an environment in which marriage has been devalued socially, legally, and spiritually, and it seems that hardly any marriage could survive a breach in the integrity of its covenant.

The inspiring story you are about to read is at the same time unique and commonplace. It is unique in its transparency as a highly visible couple takes you inside their most personal journey. It is commonplace in that thousands of couples face similar pressures on a daily basis. Many of them feel so alone with nowhere to turn for encouragement and proven truth that will rescue them from the landslide of divorce all around them.

We encourage and invite you to humbly and sincerely ask God to open your heart to the many truths and principles He would like to reveal to you through this incredible story. Truths that have faded like old watercolor paintings will yet ring true to your heart with the vibrancy of their original brilliance. You will encounter time-tested principles that are all but forgotten in a society more interested in its personal pursuit of selfish satisfaction than with righteousness that builds a foundation for the next generation.

We are both thankful to and jealous of Bob and Audrey; thankful to them for openly bringing emotional healing and hope to so many by sharing this journey of their very personal trial, torment, and triumph; jealous of them because we would have loved to have written this book. We didn't write it because it was theirs to write, and because we're busy with the next rescue and with pursuing the battle line of effective marriage ministry in the midst of a culture of divorce.

If you have a wonderful marriage, you'll be more thankful than ever once you have read this deeply moving story of marital redemption and restoration.

If you have a fair marriage that needs some reconstruction in order to become a wonderful marriage, you will find in this story reinforcement for foundations that may be slipping away.

If you have a marriage in crisis, you will find faith, hope, and love, and the boldness to shut out the naysayers and defeatists to realize that the doing of right always has its just reward.

Whatever state you find yourself in, you will be touched. So pull up the covers, settle in, block out distractions, and

## Foreword

let *Marriage Under Cover* warm your heart and soul. We look forward to the great stories that folks like you will write because your marriage has been transformed by the timeless truths contained in the following pages. May the Lord bless you with revelation knowledge, hope, ever-abounding grace, and the ability to make a difference in your situation and for others through the lessons you learn in this book.

*Leo and Molly Godzich*
*Founders of NAME – the National Association of*
*Marriage Enhancement*

# Foreword

Despite what Hollywood promotes, adultery is not entertainment—it is hell! Bob and Audrey's excellent book underlines the truth and importance of this statement. However, *Marriage Under Cover* does far more than provide diagnosis; it points to the cure for marriages infected with the deadly disease of adultery.

At first, I was reluctant to agree that Bob and Audrey should share their terribly painful story in a book. My reasoning was to protect them from further hurt since they had already suffered so much. However, I was wrong. Their courageous decision to open their lives publicly is a magnificent display of their love for our Lord in following His example to *"bind up the brokenhearted...proclaim freedom for the captives and release...for the prisoners..."* (Isaiah 61:1, NIV).

All who have gone through the pain of betrayal can identify with both Audrey and Bob in their struggle to follow our Lord's will rather than give in to their own raw and roiled emotions. Their example and wise insights offer hope and help to all in this fractured day of disposable relationships.

*Marriage Under Cover* is a poignant book written from broken hearts that are healed and being healed through the love of our Lord.

*Ron Hembree, D.Min*
*President, Cornerstone TeleVision Network*

# CHAPTER ONE

## *Concealed*

❧

Adultery.

We never dreamed it would ever happen to us. Never in our wildest imagination did we think it possible. Why would we? We had everything going for us. We had it all: a "perfect" marriage, three beautiful kids, a fruitful and fulfilling television ministry, and above all else, a deep love for Jesus. Life for us was an exciting journey filled with purpose and joy. Our course was set and our way seemed sure. The forecast: calm seas ahead. Infidelity was not even a cloud on the horizon, not even the remotest glimmer in our spirit. Or so we thought. Unknown to us, it was already headed our way, sweeping in low beneath our radar, ready to launch a sneak attack and catch us unawares.

Sin is like that. Rarely does sin post itself on a billboard and loudly announce, "Here I am!" No, our enemy employs quieter tactics. He prefers to use subtlety, subterfuge, and deception to draw us in, set us up, and when our guard is

1

down and our self-assurance up, ambush us when we least expect it.

That's how it happened with me. I was so confident—so sure—that Bob and I had what it took to stay together for-

*Sin drew me slowly but surely off the true path and onto a false trail of lies and deception.*

ever. We were in love and were sold out to Jesus and so close to Him that I *knew* we would always come through okay. I *knew* we would never go astray. Even though I never said it out loud, deep in my spirit I believed that our marriage was *immune* from adultery. How naïve! How presumptuous! That very attitude of my heart was the crack in the door that blew the thing wide open when I least expected it.

I should have seen it coming, but I didn't. My confidence in my own "immunity" is the very thing that left me completely vulnerable to infection. My pride in having an "exceptional" marriage blinded my perception.

It all began so gradually. Once the crack opened and the "hook" was in, sin drew me slowly but surely off the true path and onto a false trail of lies and self-deception. Against my conscience and my better judgment I made one small compromise, then another, and another, smugly confident that I could handle it. In my secret world, I was so busy staring at the billboard that screamed pleasure and freedom that I ignored the warning signs and never saw the deadly traps in my way until it was too late.

2

Eventually and inevitably, the unimaginable happened. Almost before I knew what I was doing, I committed the sin of adultery.

My first slight step off the path of safety was effortless and seemed completely insignificant and therefore harmless. The next was more deliberate, an exercise in self-indulgence that in time led me to the disastrous decision to believe the father of lies himself. I thought I knew my enemy until suddenly I was overtaken, brought down, and beaten to the core.

"It's no big deal," his voice inside kept telling me. "You haven't really stepped off the path; this is only a temporary detour leading to pleasure and adventure unlike anything you have ever known. Don't worry about what lies ahead. Enjoy the moment without consequence. Embrace your adventure without restraint."

Ever since I was very young I had walked the well-trodden path of truth laid out for me by my parents and by the Lord Jesus I loved. A lifetime of Christian upbringing had given me strong convictions and provided a stability that I took for granted. Stepping off into obvious evil territory was contrary to everything I believed. Yet, once I began, I continued. It was like wading into a pool of glistening water, pitch-black and perfectly lukewarm. The further I walked the deeper it got until the black waters soon surrounded my entire being. I closed my eyes, took a deep breath, and plunged in.

Self-deception really messes with the mind. During all this time, my love for Bob and my commitment to our marriage never wavered. At the same time, I wanted to keep my new secret relationship that seemed so exciting and full of adventure. In my foolishness and selfishness, I thought I could have both.

In the depths of my spirit I could still hear the faint whisper of the "still, small voice" I had grown to know and love throughout my life. That voice assured me that my "temporary detour" was actually the rushing waters of the river of death. Treacherous falls lay ahead that would cast my broken body onto the rocks of destruction below. Nevertheless, in my heart I continued relentlessly to justify my folly. After all, I was immune! Nothing could ever touch my husband, my marriage, or my family!

Finally, the solid foundation of my early life helped me see clearly the danger I was in. Disaster was rapidly approaching. Could I turn back? Could I get to the shore and find my way back to the true path? I was caught in the current! The water was getting deeper and the undertow kept pulling me down. It was hard to keep my head above water. Unless I could escape soon, I would drown.

As I forced myself to reexamine the Way that I had followed all these years, I knew what I had to do. But could I do it? At this point I recognized that survival would be nearly impossible, so I numbed myself to the ramifications. I took a deep breath and prayed for courage.

Looking back, it is amazing to see how very dark this part of the journey has been for so long. Yet, from the beginning I could always see the light. At first it was very small, only the tiniest speck, but eternally significant nonetheless. Today that same light surrounds us—me, Bob, and our children—overpowering the darkness and scattering it, bringing that black chapter of our lives to an end. Once again we face what I had come to believe was gone forever: a future of love, joy, purpose, and most of all, redemption.

Before entering this unexpected blackness, I thought I knew what pain was. In truth, I had no idea. Any pain in my life had always passed quickly. Rejection and shame were foreign to my existence. Through childhood, adolescence, parenthood, and seventeen years of marriage I had hopped and skipped through life with the freedom to fly and the confidence to laugh in the face of adversity.

*I never knew true pain until the day I confessed my adultery.*

I never knew true pain until the day I confessed my adultery and confronted the shocked reaction of the person I loved the most. The tidal wave of disbelief, horror, and anger threatened to completely envelop and choke the life out of me. In that moment I began to know pain—Bob's as well as my own—and came to the first glimmer of understanding the magnitude of my sin.

The crash of the wave bowled me over and left me swirling and turning and gasping for breath. Deafening, stifling silence. My dearest love could not speak to me. Then, suddenly, angry accusations and tormenting, probing questions that tore at my heart like a thousand knives.

Even amidst the pain I knew Jesus was with me. He didn't leave me alone to fight the storm I had created. His character of love longed to protect me from exposure and cover me. His heart of rescue and restoration carried me back to the path I knew was safe. Yet, I couldn't move. I lay on that path naked, shamed, and beaten. Only the barest spark of life still burned in me. Slowly, I opened my eyes to evaluate the damage only to discover that I could not see clearly. I needed something or someone to restore my will to live. So did Bob. We were like two people drowning in a lake, both needing rescue and neither able to help the other. In our pain, terror, and despair, our hearts cried out for help.

And help came.

On that Tuesday I was caught in a fierce internal struggle as conflicting thoughts and questions raged in the battleground of my mind. The biggest questions of all: should I tell Bob, or should I not? Deep inside I knew I had to tell. I wanted to confess, yet at the same time I didn't want to. In the end, I had no choice, really. The affair was a well-kept secret that no one else had to know about. And yet my heart told me that if I really wanted my marriage to flourish, I had to be brutally honest and expose the devastating truth. But the very thought of confession left me paralyzed with fear.

Self-deception had slowly and subtly warped my way of thinking to the point that it is a miracle that I even had the desire to tell Bob. I was so conflicted within. In the inner core of my being I wanted to do everything necessary to make up for what I had done wrong, yet on the surface of my life I wanted to continue in sin and disregard any consequences for my choices. The lies, the deception, and the indecision were tearing me apart. It was like being on a runaway train with the bridge out ahead. I knew I had to get off quickly or face destruction, but I was afraid to jump. Fear of facing reality and the pain I knew would come had kept me in my deceptions too long. Jumping off was scary beyond belief, but if I was to survive—if *we* were to survive—I had no choice. I had chosen to walk this path and now I had to choose to get off of it.

We were alone in a small office in our place of work. It was quiet and still. I was sitting on the floor holding Bob's feet. My heart was beating so fast that my hands were shaking. Somehow, slowly, I let the dreaded words escape from my mouth. Bob responded with disbelief, shock, and horror. I just sat and wept quietly. I knew my confession would hurt Bob, but I had no idea of the depth of the hurt he would suffer. In the depth of my selfishness (and adultery is, at heart, *extreme* selfishness) this whole thing had become more about me than about him. If I had realistically considered Bob's feelings in the beginning, I'm sure I wouldn't have done what I did in the first place. At any rate, I was totally unprepared for what happened next.

*I had chosen to walk this path and now I had to choose to get off of it.*

Bob stood up and walked out. He simply left the room, and I vaguely remember looking out the window and then falling onto the floor. I cupped my face in my hands and felt extremely alone. Would Bob come back? What if he didn't? If he did, what would he say? What would he do?

How could this have happened? How could such a disaster have struck our "perfect" little world? By all accounts, no one, least of all ourselves, would have pegged our marriage as one that would ever be marked by adultery. We had too much going for us. What complicated the matter for us, however, was that Bob and I didn't have "normal" jobs. Our work placed us squarely in the center of the public eye.

A few years earlier, we had started pastoring. Bob and I shared a passion for a church that would truly look and act like one big family. Our plans included eating together, hanging out together, and, of course, worshipping and learning about Jesus. We tried to imagine what church looked like in the book of Acts and pursued God's voice aggressively to escape the "box" of traditional North American church society.

It was a noble dream and actually was going amazingly well, even beyond what we had hoped for in the beginning. Our meetings were generally spontaneous, taking shape according to how we sensed the Holy Spirit leading. We worshipped without time schedules and often experienced the presence of God like nothing we had ever dreamed of before. Those few years had been a time rich in God's presence and also in our relationships with each other. Our mandate was to be a family who loved God intimately, each other openly, and the world radically.

That was one side of our lives: our "volunteer" side. Our "paying" jobs involved working with the television ministry my parents started when I was eleven years old. When I was growing up, my dad traveled extensively selling rockets on an international level. Because Dad was away a lot, Mom endured a lot of loneliness that eventually caused her to fall into deep depression. One day she reached the end of her rope and simply let go. Instead of landing into the depths, she cried out to God and landed into the reality of His presence.

From that day on everything changed. Mom and Dad both caught an infectious love for the lost and lonely. Our home became a haven for drug addicts. We held "church" in homes with barefoot hippies with their guitars and tambourines. That was *my* "70's show!"

Their passion to reach people with the "real thing" led my parents into the media. Dad quit his job with aerospace and our family began to live "by faith." In other words, we lived by a radical dependence on God's provision. I remember those days with great happiness and affection. Life was full of miracles and adventure. My two older brothers and I were challenged to believe that God does what He says He'll do and that His possibilities are limitless. Not exactly what you would call "empty" religion!

One of the miracles that occurred was in television. Without any prior media experience, Mom and Dad were given the opportunity to use a local TV studio, pay for the airtime, and run a Christian talk show. In those days there really wasn't such a thing, so it took a lot of dreaming even to envision what it would look like. A local hour-long once-a-week program quickly grew into a national daily TV show called *It's A New Day*. Guests on the show had adequate time to go deep, and the prayer line gave opportunity for one-on-one ministry.

At the time of my affair, Bob worked as the production manager of this national ministry and I co-hosted a call-in issues program that aired daily on a secular station. We were both busy in our jobs and well-known around the community. Because of our visibility to the public both in church and in television, a rescue would not be a simple matter. It never is where infidelity is concerned. Because of my foolish, selfish, sinful act, our dream world was about to come tumbling down. All our hopes and plans for the future threatened to turn to dust in our hands. At that moment, and for a long time thereafter, even our future itself seemed uncertain. It's amazing how quickly those things we take for granted as rock solid in our lives, like love, marriage, and happiness, can be shaken to their very core by one senseless act. That is when it takes all we can do just to survive. Dreams become a thing of the past.

*Because of my foolish, selfish, sinful act, our dream world was about to come tumbling down.*

Our dream had started eighteen years before.

When love first ignites, the fires of passion explode, and how well I remember the fireworks! I was away from home for the first time and only seventeen years old, but thought I had the maturity of a twenty-five-year-old. The school was incredible. Never before had I been with so many other kids my age who were as crazy about God as I was—2000 of them! And downtown Dallas, Texas, fed my hunger for adventure. Even better, my older brother Jeff was in his last semester, and I had always loved having older guys around.

This time, however, I promised myself that it would be different. I remember vowing to God that I would NOT look for a guy. Like any other girl, I dreamed regularly of the day I would meet the man of my dreams, but for now it was all about Jesus. When I got the chance to go to Bible school right after high school, I was flying high. I broke up with my boyfriend at the time because I wanted to be ready for *true* commitment to Jesus.

For the first few months, it really happened! Those days were a highlight in my spiritual walk. I looked forward to waking up every morning, praising and worshipping God. I loved my studies and all the things the Lord was doing in my life.

My brother Jeff had several roommates, and he warned every single one of them never to lay a finger on me. One of them in particular, Bob, really clicked with me simply because we were able to enjoy pure platonic friendship. We laughed, we shopped, we talked, and then we laughed some more. He began picking me up for school, and we would go out on weekends. Jeff informed me from the beginning that Bob had a fiancée in Michigan, so I knew that we would never become more than just buddies.

Although Bob had grown up in the Lutheran church, his parents later became involved in the charismatic movement. The family then moved to an Assemblies of God church so that the kids could be part of the youth group. Bob's dad was involved in Full Gospel Businessmen's Fellowship. From a young age, Bob loved to hang around with his dad and his dad's friends, especially during the many Bible studies held at their home during those years. While most other kids were out playing, Bob became a part of what his parents were doing. While still a small child he began memorizing sermons and learning how to move and speak like his Lutheran minister. Even that early in his life, Bob knew he wanted to serve in the church.

During his last two years of high school, Bob attended a private Christian school. He was also part of a gospel music

11

group that traveled through the Midwest, made several recordings, and participated in the Jesus festivals. By the time he was seventeen, Bob was the preacher of the band.

After graduation, Bob planned to attend Bible college in Minnesota, but through a providential set of circumstances wound up instead at Christ for the Nations Institute in Dallas, Texas. He was in his last semester and I in my first when we met.

One day it finally happened. Bob and I were together in my car and he was driving. I looked at him from the passenger seat and suddenly everything changed. All at once I knew that I wanted him. It was like a light turned on inside. For the first time I found myself extremely attracted to this "buddy" of mine! I said nothing and just stared straight ahead, trying to swallow this unexpected feeling.

Days and weeks went by and I kept trying to shut down this attraction to Bob. I remember walking into my apartment shouting, "I'm in love with an engaged man!" Before long, jealousy grabbed hold of me and wouldn't let go. I was so jealous of this other girl, Bob's nameless, faceless fiancée, that sometimes I couldn't think straight. And I had never even met her! I knew that the Bible said that jealousy was wrong, so I prayed constantly for victory over it. One day the Lord showed me that I had to treat it like a regular war. Every time a thought of jealousy came into my head, I combated it with the love of God and refused to "think it." The first few days were overwhelming; I felt like I was in the middle of the war of the century. Eventually, however, the jealous thoughts lost their grip, and I was free.

Meanwhile, Bob kept hanging out with me, and our friendship (as well as my love for him) grew every day.

When spring break came, Bob went home to Michigan and I returned to Winnipeg. Before he left, Bob said nothing about liking me more than a friend. Although I knew that he would see "her" again, I had an incredible peace. I also knew that this break would make us or finish us, and only time would tell. My dream was that Bob and I would get married; I loved him that much. And God knew that for the first time I had truly dedicated this relationship to Him. It was so different from any other experience I had had in the past.

*I felt like I was in the middle of the war of the century.*

When I returned to class after spring break, I saw no trace of Bob for a couple of days. I came to the conclusion that he must have chosen his commitment to the other girl. Although heartbroken, I still remained in God's peace.

Ten minutes into my counseling class one day, a big husky guy plopped down into the chair next to me. I turned my head, and there was Bob, looking directly at me with the biggest twinkle in his eyes and a huge smile on his face. He didn't have to say anything. I might be only his "buddy," but it was obvious that he was very happy to see me.

One day several weeks later, Bob confessed that he liked me "more than a buddy." I managed to choke out three words: "Yeah, me too." Within those words were months of tortured waiting and extreme ecstasy.

Could the next item on the agenda be a kiss? Not a chance. Bob and I began to dream of marriage, missions, and kids long before he ever came near me. I've always admired his wisdom, even when I didn't always understand it at the time. Everything about my relationship with Bob was so different from any other boyfriend I had ever had. And the best part...he never *was* engaged; it was just a rumor!

I don't know if it was because we waited so long, or because the chemistry between us was extreme beyond measure, but that first kiss (when it finally came) was memorable to say the least! Our love story began to take shape, and we believed that God had destined us to meet and fall in love.

That summer, Bob came home to Winnipeg with me, and we worked together in children's ministry at the ministry center. By the end of the summer, Bob had asked for my father's blessing to marry me. I was wearing a diamond ring, and we wanted to get married as soon as physically possible. At ages eighteen and twenty, we were champing at the bit. We were not only in love, we were in heat! God (and my parents!) had other plans. Mom and Dad asked us to wait for a year. Reluctantly, we agreed.

I went back to school at Christ for the Nations, and Bob went home to Michigan. This was like a test for us. Were we truly to be together or not? Would our newfound love stand the test of time and separation? It did. The next summer we reunited in Winnipeg and got married.

Every indication we could sum up said God's presence and favor was with us as a couple. We dreamed about spending the rest of our lives together. For seventeen years Bob and I continued to follow our dreams. Along the way we had three of the greatest kids any parent could hope for. Everything seemed bright. Then, suddenly, because of this stupid act, it all threatened to come crashing down in pieces around us. When I committed adultery, it was like none of our dreams mattered anymore. How can you dream when everything you have lived for is in ruins? That's what sin does. Sin is a dream stealer. It steals our dreams, our hopes, and our joy, and leaves nothing but sorrow, sadness, grief, regret, destruction, and devastation in its wake.

*God is not only a redeemer, He is a re-dreamer!*

How little we knew then of the hellish times that lay

ahead for us! Looking back from the perspective of four years later, however, the hell we went through pales in comparison to what we learned of the grace and mercy of God.

One thing we know: *not only is God a redeemer, He is a re-dreamer!*

After Bob walked out, the room was so quiet and so empty, just the way my spirit felt at that moment. Since I didn't know *how* I should feel, I cried. In fact, I made myself cry because I thought I should. Although in retrospect it seems strange to me now, this became my pattern over the next several months. I forced tears to flow, hoping they would fight through my hard heart and numbed conscience.

I knew that what I had done was wrong; that's why I had confessed to Bob. If I had kept silent, no one would have known—except me and God. But I needed to be free; I wanted to be free. Confession was my only option. Coming clean about my sin was the only way out of the deadly detour I had taken.

At the time, I had no idea of the depth of the cleansing I needed or of the depth of the destruction and devastation my adultery had caused. I didn't feel the anguish at first; I simply made a choice. I had enough of a foundation to know what was right and what was wrong and that our marriage was supposed to be forever. That was good because at the time it was the only place I could go. My repentance was just beginning, and I had no clue how long a road that process would be. As it turned out, it was a *very* long road indeed.

In the silence and loneliness I lost track of time. An hour passed, perhaps two. Then the door opened and Bob walked in. His eyes burned with a rage I had never seen before, an anger so intense that it lashed out and struck me with almost the force of a physical blow. As his eyes bored into me like hot coals, Bob said in a tight voice, "I called Leo Godzich."

When Audrey told me she had committed adultery, it was like a blow to the stomach. My first, instantaneous response was disbelief: *No, this can't be happening. I can't have heard her right. I must have misunderstood her; surely she didn't say what I think she said.* As the reality hit home—as I realized deep in my gut that it *was* true—I was completely devastated. How could this have happened? What had Audrey done to me? To us? To our marriage? To our children? To our future? All of a sudden, the bottom fell out of my life. Nothing made sense anymore. The whole scenario was like a scene from some surrealistic movie. As the questions arose, so did my anger. I needed to do something, and fast, but I didn't know what. Finally, I simply walked out of the room, leaving Audrey alone with the bombshell she had dropped right into the middle of our marriage. I needed time to be alone and do—what?

*What should I do? Where should I go?* My first impulse was to run; to go somewhere—anywhere—to get away from where I was; to get away from Audrey and the horrible reality that I could not yet face. The urge to run is the instinctive response of anyone suddenly faced with danger or disaster. *Maybe if I run as far away from this as I can, I will be able to sort things out and then be able to come back and reenter.* As reasonable as that may sound, there is only one problem: *it doesn't work.* The only thing that running accomplishes is to greatly prolong the healing process—if it occurs at all.

> *When we are wounded, that is the time to seek help, not solitude.*

I bow-hunted for a season and learned that the first thing a deer does when it has been struck a death blow is to run. It seeks a place to hide and bed down and heal itself. There it will stay and die. So often, when we get hit or wounded or broken, all we want to do is break away from everyone else and be alone. All that lies at the end of that road is death; perhaps not physical death, but at least the death of the relationship. When we are wounded, that is the time to seek help, not solitude. If we run, we risk losing everything.

My next impulse was to tell everybody I saw about what had happened, to broadcast my innocence and to point to Audrey as the evil one who offended and betrayed her husband. It was like I had lost my strong right arm. I was one bloody mess. Everything inside me wanted to blast out publicly at Audrey. I wanted to justify my case. I wanted everyone to know, before anything else happened, how good *I* was, and how right *I* was and how wrong and how bad Audrey was. I wanted to shout: *"See what she did to me!"* The only thing that would have accomplished was to spread blood everywhere, making a mess of people who didn't need to be part of the mess. It would have been awful.

Of course, I was not thinking this clearly about my options right after I walked out on Audrey. I was in a total quandary, absolutely clueless about what to do and unable to make decisions on my own. All I knew was that I needed help and I needed it fast. I went into my office, shut the door, and immediately pulled a book from my shelf. Its title was *Is God in Your Marriage?* A man named Leo Godzich had written it.

Several years earlier, Leo and his wife Molly had been guests on *It's a New Day!* Audrey and I had hosted that particular program. Even though we had all hit it off together that morning, we did not know each other well and had not kept in touch. What suddenly drew me to Leo's book and to his name? A desperate man grasping at even the smallest straw of hope, the merest thread that might somehow pull him to safety.

Looking back on it now, I realize that something else was at work as well. In the weeks immediately following Audrey's confession, we discovered that anybody we told of our situation had an opinion on what we should do. But God wasn't interested in man's opinion. Unknown to me (or Audrey) at the time, God already had a rescue mission in place for us and it involved Leo Godzich and the church family at Phoenix First Assembly. Nothing takes God by surprise. He was not in shock like we were. He knew we needed vessels of His peace and wisdom to get us through those first bewildering weeks and those first difficult decisions, but mostly to see us through the initial pain.

Almost in a daze I pulled Leo's phone number in Phoenix, Arizona, from the ministry information at the back of his book, dialed it, and waited anxiously as the call rang through.

*Voice mail.*

I couldn't believe it. He wasn't there. Here I was in crisis, and Leo was at lunch! All I could do was leave a message. Then I sat in my office with my back to the door and waited. And waited. And waited. Finally, Leo's secretary called me back. When I introduced myself and explained my connection with Leo, she said that she remembered me and told me how much Leo and Molly had loved being on the show with us. She was so sweet and loving. I was raw and bloody, and I'm afraid I cut her off rather rudely. "Okay," I said, "here's what's going on. I need to talk to Leo right away. I just found out that my wife had an affair."

Although still sweet and loving, her tone changed at the gravity of my message. She assured me that Leo would call me back as soon as possible.

I waited some more. Finally, the phone rang again. It was Leo. I quickly filled him in on the situation. Leo immediately recognized that I needed someone to guide me through this minefield because I was in no condition to find my own way. Right away he gave me very strict instructions on what to do and what not to do. The big question was: "Who else knows about this? Do your children know?" They didn't, and Leo said they did not need to know. Instantly, he concealed the matter. Gently but firmly, Leo took control and spoke to us with biblical truth and understanding.

"What do I do, Leo?"

*I needed someone to guide me through this minefield because I was in no condition to find my own way.*

"The first thing you do is get back into that bed with Audrey tonight. Don't spend one night apart from each other. Not one."

I couldn't believe it. "You've got to be kidding!"

"I'm not saying you have to have sex, but you will not defile that marriage bed. Do not sleep apart. That is a *vital* principle because you are not going to be a part of this divorce culture. The mathematics of marriage is not addition, but *multiplication: not* one plus one equals two, but *one times one equals one!* You and Audrey are husband and wife. You are one flesh. This is your marriage; get in there and fight for it. The enemy is a divider. In fact, the New Testament Greek word for 'devil' is *diabole*, a mathematical term that means 'one that divides the whole in half.' Don't give in to the emotions that would drive you apart. Do the right thing. Stay with Audrey tonight."

I did go back to bed with Audrey that night, and it is one of the hardest things I have ever done. One thing's for sure; I slept on the very edge of the bed. Guaranteed, there was no spooning going on that night!

As for my second impulse—to tell everyone what Audrey had done—Leo nipped that one in the bud as well. If I had followed my emotions at the time, raw as they were, the result would have been disastrous. In my confusion I thought that if I ran, Audrey would be exposed; if I spoke up, others would know what had happened and Audrey would be forced to confess. She would become the villain, and I would be justified. I wanted to gather an army for me and against her.

That's the danger of self-righteousness. When someone hurts us, pride swells up in our defense and calls attention to all the offender's shortcomings while at the same time blinding us to our own faults. I was hurt and angry, and in my anger and injured pride I wanted to hurt back. At that moment I wanted the whole world to know just how wrong Audrey was and how wronged I was.

Leo never gave me that chance. Not for a single moment did he ever coddle my bruised image or give me the opportunity to wallow in self-pity. Not for a single moment did he feel sorry for me or allow me to feel sorry for myself. There was no "Poor Bob, I can't believe she did that to you." Instead, he gave me a dose of hard reality. "Bob, I know you feel like your flesh is ripped open. I know you are raw and wounded and bleeding. I know you feel devastated. But the question is, what are you going to do about it? Are you going to run, or are you going to stay and be an instrument of God's healing in this marriage? Are you going to expose this thing and blow it up so that it brings down even more destruction just so you can justify your own self righteousness? Or are you going to protect and *cover* your wife and children? Are you going to *cover* your marriage?"

Those were tough words that were hard for me to swallow, but they shocked me into thinking more rationally again, or at least outside of myself. I realized I had to really watch where I was going. In my pain and anger, I was extremely vulnerable to the lies of the enemy that said, "You're the only person who has ever gone through something like this. No one else understands. No one else cares. Nobody wants to listen. You're on your own, buddy." Our immature nature always looks for someone who will comfort us and make us feel good. I wanted somebody to stroke me and say, "Bob, you were a great husband. You don't deserve this. I can't believe this happened to you. You were so gracious, so gentle, kind and giving; you did all the right things." That's what I wanted to hear.

Leo would have none of it. Instead, he quickly spoke the truth of Proverbs 25:2 over our situation: *"It is the glory of God to conceal a matter, but the glory of kings is to search out a matter."* God wanted to conceal the matter of this crisis in our lives, not to hide it away where it would fester and become infected, but for healing. Whenever we cut ourselves, our first response usually is to cover the wound with antiseptic and a bandage. This protects the injured area and promotes healing.

In the same way, concealing the matter concerning me and Audrey was not to cover it *up*, but to *cover* it so that healing could take place. Leo informed me that despite my feelings of the moment, it was my responsibility to *cover* Audrey rather than expose her. It was my responsibility to *cover* my children. At this point, everything was on a strict "need-to-know" basis, and our children did not need to know. If I had followed my impulse and blurted everything out at the beginning, I would have played right into the enemy's hands. It would have been like setting off a bomb in a crowded market. The devastation and destruction would have been immense. Thanks to Leo, that never happened. The explosion was contained. By the grace and mercy of a loving God, the matter was concealed.

*Concealing the matter was not to cover it up, but to cover it so that healing could take place.*

Through a strength beyond our own, Audrey and I made it through that first night—*together*.

God understood the intense pain that both Audrey and I were experiencing. He knew that we were in no state to help each other at that point. We could not identify with each other's pain because our own pain was too great. By covering and concealing the matter, the Lord protected us from that until we were ready. That's the way God works. He meets us where we are and ministers healing in that place so that He can take us to new levels of healing, growth, and understanding.

Leo may have hit me pretty hard, but he didn't let Audrey off the hook either. He told her that the first thing she needed to do was tell her parents.

I told my parents the next day. Next to confessing to Bob, confessing to my parents that I had committed adultery was the hardest thing I have ever done. The pain was indescribable, yet I had to do it. After all, my parents were my heroes. I had spent my life trying to make them happy. I had always hoped that my adult life would be a harvest of fruit from the seeds they had lovingly planted in me from the beginning. They didn't deserve this any more than Bob did. It should never have happened in the first place, and confessing my sin to my parents was a harsh reality for all of us. We were not talking about some little fling of selfishness that led me temporarily off the beaten path, but a cataclysmic, foundation-shaking event that would forever alter life as we knew it.

I sat down with Mom and Dad separately and told them what I had done. How I wished at that moment that I could turn back the clock and have another chance to make the right choices! As I poured out the truth to each of them, I saw the intense hurt in their eyes. My face grew hot just as it did when I confessed to Bob. Although I couldn't see it then, I know now that their pain was not just sorrow and disappointment that I had let them down—as real as that was—but pain at the knowledge of what lay ahead for me.

All loving parents want to protect their children from pain, and my parents were no exception. Their love was deep and unchanging. But they also recognized that they could not shield me from the pain or consequences of my sin. They could not protect me from the future. Mom and Dad were wise to the ways of life and could see, much more than I could, the ramifications of my actions.

I asked them to forgive me and they did. Mom and Dad each separately reassured me that their love was unconditional and that they would do anything humanly possible to get us through this crisis. Beyond that, our words were few. We were sitting in the living room of our home. The air was thick, the silence stifling, and the sense of loss piercingly acute. It was as though someone had died and nobody knew what to say.

The silence didn't last long. Bob's pain and anger finally spilled over into a tidal wave of emotion flung in my direction. Suddenly, it was all about questions. Bob already knew the "who" of the affair. Now he demanded to know when and where and how many times. He wanted to know if I enjoyed it and if I loved this other man. He was painfully obsessed with knowing every sordid detail of my infidelity, and I can't blame him. I had betrayed his trust and violated the sanctity of our marriage vows. His confident assurance of my love for him had been severely damaged.

Although Bob never hit me or abused me physically in any way, his incessant barrage of angry questions began to feel like it. Each question, each probe for yet another detail, left me feeling smaller and smaller. Emotionally, I was torn down and beaten up. In my own mind I became completely insignificant as a person and felt my sense of value shrinking and flowing away.

With every new confession I tried to appease Bob's mind, but I knew my answers were not what he wanted to hear. Bob was grasping at straws, yearning to hear anything from me that would give him hope. He wanted to hear me say that it was not my fault or that I had no control. He desperately wanted to believe that I was a helpless victim and not a willing participant. That way he would have an excuse to release me from responsibility and could focus all of his wrath on the "other" man. I *wanted* to lie to make everything all right. I *wanted* to minimize what happened and escape the torture. In all truthfulness, however, I could not give Bob the answers he was looking for. I was responsible, and I knew it. Denying it would only prolong the pain and diminish our chances of healing. Only the truth—the harsh, unvarnished truth—would do any good now.

*The repercussions of my sin had catapulted me headlong into an arena of death and destruction.*

I never expected Bob to physically hurt me, but in my own guilt and pain I reached the point where I wanted him to. I began to crave physical punishment to bring just fulfillment to my sin. All of my emotional pain and fear begged for a physical manifestation. More than once I imagined taking a knife and cutting into my legs. I remember sitting in Bob's office, his hurt and angry eyes penetrating right into my very soul in a look so destructive that it sent shivers down my spine. I literally could not absorb another moment, so I began digging my thumbnail into my hand until the blood started to run.

Again and again I asked myself how life had taken such a turn. Only a few short months before I had been a happy, confident woman secure in the love of God and of her family. Now, the repercussions of my sin had catapulted me headlong into an arena of death and destruction where losing everything I held dear loomed as a very real possibility. For the first time in my life I truly understood what David the psalmist felt when he wrote:

*My heart is severely pained within me, and the terrors of death have fallen upon me. Fearfulness and trembling have come upon me, and horror has overwhelmed me. So I said, "Oh, that I had wings like a dove! I would fly away and be at rest. Indeed, I would wander far off, and remain in the wilderness. Selah. I would hasten my escape from the windy storm and tempest"* (Psalm 55:4-8).

At the time Bob first contacted him, Leo was involved in a pastor's conference in Phoenix that was sponsored by his church. Despite his busy schedule, Leo knew that Bob and I shouldn't be alone. He insisted that we fly to Phoenix where his church would put us up for the week and he would talk with us as he could.

One of my cousins is an airline pilot, and she graciously made two complimentary tickets available to us, not knowing, of course, the real reason we needed them. We made hasty arrangements for our children to stay with my parents. Finally, the day after I confessed my adultery to Bob, on the evening of the same day I told my parents, Bob and I boarded a flight to Phoenix, Arizona.

What lay ahead? God alone knew.

# Chapter Two

# A Desperate Housewife

How could a committed Christian woman—and a happy, happy-go-lucky, and happily married wife and mother—with a very public ministry fall into the sin of adultery? What could cause such a thing?

Unfortunately, this is not as rare a problem as we might think. To one degree or another, all of us are influenced by the culture in which we live. Sometimes subtly and sometimes blatantly, our culture imprints its views, values, and mores on our minds. Mental imprints become thoughts, and thoughts pondered long enough morph into actions.

Let's face it, modern western society encourages infidelity. Look at what has happened to the general perception of moral values. Not too many years ago, most people in western society were in general agreement on basic moral standards that characterized an enlightened and civilized people. Not anymore. In today's "anything goes" world, truth and morality are in the eye of the beholder and what may be moral and right for you may not be moral and right for your neighbor. There is no absolute truth, no absolute standard upon which to establish any meaningful system of moral or ethical behavior.

*Modern western society encourages infidelity.*

Traditional views of marriage and the family are being undermined more and more every day. The time-honored nuclear family of a husband and wife under one roof with their children is under vigorous assault by those who wish to redefine the family to mean any union that establishes a "household" of any kind, whether involving multiple partners, same-sex partners, or the so-called "open marriage" where marital partners willingly and knowingly seek out other relationships as well. The current effort among many to legalize and legitimize homosexual "marriage" in Canada and the United States exemplifies the present state of affairs.

If there is no absolute moral standard, and if marriage and family can be anything we want them to be, then what is the value of faithfulness to *one* partner? Everything is relative and all of life boils down to the simple maxim: *it's all about me.*

Modern western society encourages unfaithfulness. Adultery is the very epitome of selfishness, but look at our culture. Every aspect of our contemporary consumer culture is built around instant self-gratification: whatever you want, you deserve to have it *right now*. If you can't afford it, charge it. If it feels good, do it. If you are unsatisfied or unhappy in one relationship, simply drop it and move on to another one. Keep moving until you find one that satisfies you. After all, life is all about what makes *you* feel good, what works for *you*, what will help *you* advance toward achieving all of *your* personal goals.

Adultery is also an act of desperation. Ours is a desperate culture filled with desperate people; people desperately seeking some shred of meaning, purpose, and happiness in a society that cannot provide them. Occasionally, this desperation flares up and manifests itself in dramatic and terrible acts of violence, such as workplace or schoolyard shootings or incidents of "road rage." More often than not, however, the desperation of our age remains behind the scenes, concealed behind the partitions of our office cubicles or contained within the walls of our homes. Henry David Thoreau was right when he wrote, "the mass of men lead lives of quiet desperation." Day after day, week in and week out, millions of people endure dead-end jobs and unfulfilling careers, constantly pursuing the acquisition of "things" and then wonder why they have never found the contentment they seek. Many of them eventually stop trying and simply accept their lot with resignation, which Thoreau calls "confirmed desperation."

What was true of Thoreau's nineteenth century world is just as true of ours in the twenty-first century. *We live in a culture of quiet desperation.*

Nowhere is this truer than in the area of our relationships. Our society is obsessed with beauty, romance, and forbidden love. The worlds of fashion design and advertising hold up the supermodel as an impossible standard of "beauty" against which all women are pressured to compare themselves and conform to. Little wonder then that cases of anorexia nervosa and bulimia among women continue to rise.

Illicit romance and forbidden love are regular storylines in movies and on television. Our airwaves (and our minds) are saturated with sex. Men and women hop in and out of bed with each other as easily as they change clothes. The entire plots of some shows are nothing more than discussions of various sexual conquests, dreamed-of sexual conquests, or attempted sexual conquests. *Sex and the City* takes middle-aged career women and makes them "hot" and ready for real love. Unfortunately they never find it. In *The Door in the Floor*, Kim Basinger plays a beautiful woman who, cursed with a pathetic husband, pursues a relationship with a younger man. The title of one of the newest and most popular dramas on television in recent days says it all: *Desperate Housewives*.

Many married women today live in a private fantasy world their husbands know nothing about, a world in which they crave mystery, adventure, and forbidden love. The epidemic of middle-aged women falling for younger men has crazed our society, but no one is telling the other side—the dark side—of the story: the consequences of infidelity in the destruction of marriages and the devastation of families. Desperately seeking happiness and fulfillment, they follow what they think is their heart's true desire, only to end up broken, lonely, destitute, and empty.

The picture is not much better for married men. Many middle-aged men are either lazy and depressed or angry and overworked. Somewhere along the way in the daily grind of making a living, they have lost their sense of purpose and adventure and have given up on their dreams.

Between the demands of the workplace and confusion over their roles as men in a rapidly changing culture, they become numbed to the needs, hopes, and dreams of their wives and children. Such men need to learn how to love again, not just in the natural, but in *supernatural* love, where they will rediscover the true adventure they long for.

> *"Forbidden love" is a dead-end road that leads only to heartache and destruction.*

"Forbidden love," whatever form it takes, is a dead-end road that leads only to heartache and destruction. Signposts along the way may promise adventure, excitement, and satisfaction, but they are lies. Contrary to the messages that fill our airwaves, and in defiance of our modern secular culture, husbands and wives everywhere need to learn to find intrigue in *each other* and rediscover that everything they are looking for is right there under their own roof.

Adultery is *still* an ugly thing, despite the attempts of contemporary western society to downplay it. Many people today "wink" at the "naïve" and "prudish" moral sensibilities such as found in Nathaniel Hawthorne's *The Scarlet Letter*, in which the adulterous Hester Prynne is required to wear a bright red "A" on her breast as an emblem of her public disgrace. If modern media are to be believed, today's "Hester Prynnes" should wear the "scarlet letter" not as a token of sin and shame but as a badge of freedom, enlightenment, and even honor. According to these cultural icons, infidelity carries no stigma, produces no consequences, and leaves no guilt.

The truth, however, is far different. Adultery is a vicious beast that rips the heart out of a marriage, rends families apart, and leaves everyone touched by it torn and bleeding in its wake. Infidelity touches many more of us than we probably have any idea of. This is especially true in our internet age with the easy availability and ever-expanding proliferation of pornography and other sex-related sites on the worldwide web. One study by the Harding Institute reported over 72,000 sexually explicit sites on the internet with as many as 266 new porn sites being added every *day*. These new sites alone generated annual revenue in excess of one billion dollars.[1]

According to The National Coalition for the Protection of Children and Families, approximately 40 million people in the United States (out of a current population of around 290 million) are sexually involved with the internet. That's almost one out of every seven Americans.[2] Twenty-five per-cent of all search engine requests are pornography-related.[3] Another study by the American Academy of Matrimonial Lawyers revealed a growing number of divorce cases nationwide brought on by one spouse's addiction to internet pornography.[4]

Wait a minute! We were talking about adultery, weren't we, not internet pornography? Isn't there a difference?

Essentially, no. Like every other sin, adultery begins in the mind. It begins as a single unclean thought, an unholy desire, or the gratification of an inappropriate urge. Unchecked, such thoughts, desires, and urges tend to take on more tangible form through surfing porn sites on the internet, picking up pornographic magazines or books, or watching pornographic movies. Once the mind-set is there and the practice established, it is only a small step to physical, sexual infidelity. Thought precedes but leads to action, and in the judgment of God, the two are the same. Jesus said that a man who looks at a woman to lust after her has *already* committed adultery with her in his heart (Matthew 5:28).

*Like every other sin, adultery begins in the mind.*

This relationship between thought and action is borne out in experience. A growing body of evidence supports a high correlation between online infidelity (such as sex chat rooms) and subsequent real time sexual affairs. Online sex relaxes inhibitions, accelerates a sense of intimacy, and encourages bold cybernetic sexual "behavior" that can then easily transfer over into physical infidelity.[5]

Accurate statistics on adultery are hard to obtain because of the sensitivity of the topic. One recent national study by the University of California, San Francisco, found that twenty-four percent of men and fourteen percent of women have had sex outside their marriages.[6] In actuality, the percentages are probably much higher, particularly if we include the instances of "mental" or "soulical" adultery that have not yet reached the physical stage. Professional counselor Janis Abrahms Spring, author of a book called *After the Affair*, says that affairs affect one out of every 2.7 couples.[7]

Studies as long ago as the late 1980s indicated that by the age of forty, as many as fifty to sixty-five percent of men and forty-five to fifty-five percent of women have had at least one extramarital affair.[8] With the changes in society since then, as well as the increasing number both of women in the workforce and women engaging in internet relationships, the percentage of women who have affairs is now very likely closer to that of men.[9]

> *Adultery is a desperate act by a desperate person.*
>
>

Infidelity is a genuine, alarming, and growing problem that affects almost every one of us, and it carries serious consequences socially, morally, emotionally, and spiritually.

Adultery is a desperate act by a desperate person. That's the dangerous thing about desperation—it is unpredictable. No one, least of all the desperate person, ever knows what will happen.

*Desperate people often do shocking things...without notice.*

Quite often, desperation is born out of a sense of *lack*. Something seems to be missing in our life, but we don't know exactly what. The more we think about it, the more we realize that the zest for life, or the excitement and sense of adventure, are gone. Perhaps we become dissatisfied with our job or with the amount of money we make or with the house we are living in. We begin to feel that we don't have everything we want or need. Our natural tendency is to seek to satisfy our lack by acquiring more "stuff," thinking that more money or more possessions or a nicer car or a bigger house will make us happy.

Such a sense of lack is one of Satan's most potent and effective deceptions. He loves to plant in our minds seeds of discontent that cause us to focus not on what we have but on what we don't have: "I need this...I don't have that...I want to be happy...I want to have peace and joy in my life." There is certainly nothing wrong with desiring happiness, peace, and joy, but the problem comes when we search for them in the wrong places or seek them through inappropriate means. The enemy continually starves our hearts with this sense of lack, just as he did to Eve in the Garden of Eden: "God is holding out on you, Eve. There's something more that He is not telling you; something more that He has not given you." He calls into question the character of God. Satan continues to use this strategy today because it works. We humans of the twenty-first century are just as prone to this lie as Eve was so long ago.

This deep-rooted sense of lack in our lives will drive us one of two ways. First, it may draw us into all types of sin where we seek to fill our lack through alcohol or drugs or the reckless pursuit of pleasure. We may seek fulfillment through wrong or inappropriate relationships. Frustrated by life, we may simply throw up our arms and turn to the ways of the world, even to self-destructive behavior, just to fill the void in our life. Remember, desperate people do shocking things.

Second, if we have a spiritual bent, our sense of lack can lead to legalism. Lacking any real sense of joy or peace or fulfillment in our relationship with God, we try to compensate with a set of rules and regulations that we expect to produce in us perfect peace, satisfaction, and joy. In reality, these rules simply drive us farther away from the righteousness of Christ. Seeking our own righteousness, we pledge to do everything right, hoping somehow to find that relationship with God by something we do. It doesn't work.

Desperate people do shocking things without notice. Some of the most desperate people in the world are married people, and often they don't even know it. Many married women are desperate for admiration, attention, and appreciation. The daily grind of juggling kids, career, and home can easily become overwhelming, leaving them extremely tired and busy, yet bored and with little time for themselves. This was me, and yet I would not have identified these longings within myself.

Making matters worse, their husbands are busy too, and often so preoccupied with work-related issues that they don't pick up on their wives' need for affirmation. For whatever reason, few men really know how to love their wives extravagantly and unconditionally. Many of them have lost their vision and their sense of purpose and without these, they lack drive, and think a little blue pill will fix it.

Women are looking for men with vision, purpose, and drive. Wives are looking for these qualities they once saw in their husbands but which seem to have disappeared. They wonder what happened to the man of adventure they married. Their "knight in shining armor" is looking rather tarnished.

Husbands, on the other hand, are looking for their wives to keep up the home, keep up their appearance, and be responsive to their husbands' needs. Tired and busy women sometimes let the housework slide and let themselves go and then wonder why their husbands no longer seem attracted to them.

These are the kinds of thoughts, feelings, and attitudes among married people that often sow seeds that will sprout later and grow into the wild weed of infidelity. As a husband's or wife's perceived needs—real or imagined—go unmet, a quiet desperation begins to grow in their spirit, a desperation they may not even consciously recognize, yet one that drives them to look elsewhere to meet their needs. When this state of affairs exists, an adulterous relationship becomes a very real and dangerous possibility.

*Natural love is not enough to build and sustain a godly and protected marriage.*

One reason this happens with so many married couples is because of the unrealistic expectations they bring into the relationship to start with. Many people enter marriage looking to their spouse to fulfill their own needs. That is how they define love, even if they are not consciously aware of it. They have needs that they expect their spouse to meet. When it doesn't happen, disappointment sets in, which leads eventually to discontent and restlessness. They begin to feel trapped in an unsatisfying relationship, and the longer they feel trapped the more desperate they become until they are ready to do anything—even commit adultery—to get free.

Natural love is not enough to build and sustain a godly and protected marriage. Spouses must learn to love each other *supernaturally* through the power of the Spirit of God. This involves learning *not* to see our spouse as our *answer* or as the one to meet *our* needs but to look to Jesus as the source and supplier of all that we both need. A husband and wife should be each other's "best friend" on earth, but each should also have an even greater friendship with Christ.

There is another root of infidelity in marriage that is even more insidious and dangerous than unrealistic expectations: an impure thought and fantasy life.

Men are aroused sexually primarily through visual stimulation, which is why internet pornography is more of a problem for them than it is for women. (However, the number of women becoming addicted to online sex, whether visual sites or chat rooms, is also on the rise.) For many men, whether single or married, visual pornography is the jumping-off point for a vivid fantasy life in which they imagine having sex with the women they see in the pictures. With the more explicit, hardcore pornography, they often participate in vicarious sex by watching it performed in the pictures or on the videos. It is very easy for married men to transfer their sexual fantasies to the marriage bed, imagining all sorts of "hot" or "forbidden" scenarios while having sex with their wives, even to the point sometimes of fantasizing that they are having sex with somebody else.

Because men are so easily aroused sexually, and because so many men have a very active sexual fantasy life, they are routinely depicted as the "culprit" when sexual dysfunction arises in a marriage. Although there may be some validity in this, wives are not off the hook. Many women, and particularly married women, are addicted to trashy romance novels, soap operas, and fantasy. The dark and dirty secret of our culture is that women by and large have just as active and just as vivid a sexual fantasy life as men. The problem is so pervasive that it is safe to say that many women, as much as eighty percent of the time when they are with their husbands, are thinking about someone else.

Like men, women, too, are caught up in the mental game of imagining "hot," "forbidden," or "naughty" sexual scenarios in order to work themselves up to an "appropriate" degree of sexual arousal to satisfy either themselves or their husbands. Many, many wives feel they have to do something "bad," at least in their minds, in order to be good in the bedroom. Few women have the sexual drive that men do, and *this is normal.* Most women, however, truly want to satisfy their husbands sexually and to be satisfied themselves, and they will resort to whatever it takes to make it happen. If that means imagining an illicit sexual encounter or acting out in their minds a particularly erotic scene from their latest romance novel, then so be it.

> *Sexual fantasy is a serious problem for both men and women in our society.*

Someone might ask, "What's the big deal with sexual fantasies? As long as I am with my spouse and not someone else, what does it matter if I use fantasy to get aroused?" The problem is that by doing so, we settle for a marriage relationship that is less than what God desires for us, a relationship in which our thinking has been tainted and corrupted by worldly attitudes and assumptions. We also aren't living in pure truth. And there is always power, blessing, and anointing where there is truth.

Sexual fantasy is a serious problem for both men and women in our society, a problem made even worse by the fact that so few people even recognize that it *is* a problem.

Fantasies about sex have become so prevalent in our minds that we take them for granted. They are virtually second nature to us. We have been caught up in these thoughts and imaginings for so long that we assume that such fantasies are a *natural* and *normal* part of our sexuality. In reality, these thoughts and imagined scenarios amount to committing adultery in our heart, which is *not* how God intended our marriages to be.

God's desire for our marriages is that we find complete and total fulfillment—mentally, emotionally, and physically—with our spouse and no one else. In God's eyes, mental, emotional and "soulical" adultery is just as serious as physical adultery. As it says in Proverbs, *"Let your fountain be blessed, and rejoice with the wife of your youth. As a loving deer and a graceful doe, let her breasts satisfy you at all times; and always be enraptured with her love"* (Proverbs 5:18-19). God designed marriage in such a way that spouses who follow His design can find complete and total fulfillment in each other without resorting to imaginary and fantastic scenarios.

Since Bob and I first began telling our story at seminars and conferences, we have discovered just how prevalent this problem of sexual imagination and fantasy really is, even among Christians. Whenever we start to talk about this subject, inevitably the room falls completely silent and we have everyone's undivided attention. Why? Because this subject hits home. It is one of the great, undiscussed secrets among believers. Nobody wants to admit that impure thoughts and sexual fantasies are a problem in the Christian community. It is there and it is very real, but no one wants to talk about it. Everybody is so afraid that nobody but them wrestles with these things.

42

Whenever I start to share my own experiences in this area, I can feel every woman in the room thinking, *"Oh, my gosh, she's reading my mind!"* In the ministry time that follows, there are always many women in the group who can't get into the prayer line fast enough in order to receive prayer over this very issue. When it comes to our thought and fantasy life, women need deliverance as much as men do.

Part of the reason I ended up in adultery was because I had been living with these kinds of things most of my life—and all my adult and married life—but was barely aware of them. Even some of my earliest childhood memories are sexual in nature, which is completely contrary to my character and upbringing. I grew up believing that one of God's gifts to me was purity, so when these other thoughts came, they confused me. Always there was this back and forth in my mind between the pure and the impure. Eventually I accepted it all as part of my identity. I was wrong to do this, and in doing so, I gave in to the enemy's plot.

During the first seventeen years of my marriage, the pattern of my sexual thoughts seemed innocent to me. I wouldn't have admitted a problem about them even to my very best friend because I never recognized it as a problem myself. Bob was totally unaware. I routinely fantasized scenarios that made our lovemaking "forbidden" and it added excitement for me. In my mind, I always justified it with the excuse, "At least I'm with my husband." My thoughts were closely associated with my actions. I now understand that my situation bordered on an addiction.

My experiences talking and praying with women at various conferences and meetings has convinced me that I am not alone in this struggle. Far from it. I believe that the problem of an impure thought and fantasy life, particularly among Christian women, is far more widespread and deeply rooted than any of us would care to admit. The struggles of men in this area are more widely known and publicized, but with women it is generally still a guarded subject.

*The problem of an impure thought and fantasy life is far more wide-spread and deeply rooted than any of us care to admit.*

The problem for married couples is that even though men and women both struggle with their thought lives in regard to sex, they won't admit the problem to themselves, much less talk about it with each other. Instead, they simply continue on with a relationship that is less than what they dreamed and hoped for, never understanding the problem but trying to make the best of the situation. Many times, as with me and Bob, they may enjoy a very happy and fulfilling relationship in every way and yet be unaware that their thought life and mental habits have left their marriage unprotected and vulnerable to attack in a critical area.

Satan has lied to us all our lives, and we have bought into his lies. He tells us that we're unlovable or that we're inadequate or that we're not sexy enough or attractive enough by ourselves to hold the interest and attention of our spouse. We need something "extra" to boost our appeal. Our society doesn't help with its false standards of beauty and sexiness and its consumer-driven materialism that links our attractiveness and personal worth to how we dress, how we look, and how much "stuff" we own rather than on our spirit, integrity, and character.

*It doesn't have to be this way.* God created all of us with the capacity for very beautiful and pure-minded sex with our spouses. The first thing we have to do is acknowledge the lies about ourselves that we have believed and that have held us in bondage. Only by recognizing those lies for what they are can we let go of them and receive deliverance. Next, we must relearn how to think: develop new thought patterns and processes and, as Romans 12:2 says, *"be transformed by the renewing of* [our] *mind."*

> *Change can be difficult and is frequently painful, particularly when we have to face up to unpleasant truths about ourselves.*

The first step, acknowledging the lies, is not always easy. For one thing, long-ingrained mental habits can be hard to break and, for another, deception usually does not give way readily. Sometimes it is easier to stay in deception than to move from deception to truth. Change can be difficult and is frequently painful, particularly when we have to face up to unpleasant truths about ourselves. But we need to remember that these unclean thoughts do not define who we are.

~=~

In my case, it took a long time to reach the place where I truly understood the depth of my self-deception. Only in the last year or so—three years after my adultery and the beginning of the healing and restoration process—have I become free from the lies and deception that had gripped me since childhood. That deliverance could not come until I recognized the true nature and source of the problem.

One night Bob and I were spending some time with a man named Henry Wright and his wife. Henry is the author of a book entitled *The More Excellent Way*, which deals with the subject of physical healing and the spiritual roots of sin that cause sickness. We shared with Henry and his wife a five-minute "condensed version" of what happened to us.

Henry looked at me and said, "You know why you did that, don't you?"

"Not really," I replied. "I have some ideas, but to tell you the truth, I am more confused about it than anything else."

"What I believe happened," said Henry, "is that an unclean spirit attached itself to you, possibly when you were born, and has been speaking lies to you all your life. You always assumed these thoughts were your own. You have listened to them and, over the years, you came to agree with them. Audrey, you have had these thoughts in your mind, but they do not identify who you really are. Those thoughts do not originate with you but come from the unclean spirit that is lying to you."

Henry helped me understand that it was the unclean spirit that told me that I had to take my thoughts into a "forbidden zone" in order to achieve sexual satisfaction; I had to think of something "bad" in order to have a good experience. That was my problem for the first seventeen years of my marriage. I never got into porn or romance novels or anything like that, but I convinced myself that I had to think of a "bad" scenario before I could have satisfying sex or (so I thought) before I could satisfy Bob.

In the seventh chapter of Romans, Paul talks about how he does the things he doesn't want to do and does not do the things he wants to do and knows he should do. He goes on to explain that it is sin rising up in him that causes him to act differently from what he desires in his heart. Finally, after recognizing that he is helpless to help himself, he praises God for the deliverance he has received in Christ.

In the same way, this unclean spirit would speak into my spirit, my spirit would agree, I would yield, and the unclean spirit would rise up and proceed to do exactly what it wanted to do. This was a demonic principality with a distinct personality that had chosen me in which to live out its evil purpose. This reminds me of the foundational truth: *"For we do not wrestle against flesh and blood, but against principalities, against powers, against the rulers of the darkness of this age, against spiritual hosts of wickedness in the heavenly places"* (Ephesians 6:12).

Once I understood the problem—an unclean spirit—all I wanted was to be delivered of it. For the last several years I had focused hard on *starving* that fantasy mind-set by *"bringing every thought into captivity to the obedience of Christ"* as 2 Corinthians 10:5 says, and trying not to allow any unclean thoughts to take hold. But this wasn't true freedom—it was striving. Once I understood the true nature of my enemy, my attitude changed. Why starve the unclean spirit when I could be delivered of it? I received deliverance that night.

*The enemy is always watching and ready to exploit our tiniest weakness.*

This was a big deal for me. For the first time I separated myself from this sin and identified its origin. I knew I wanted to be pure, and I wanted to love God and Bob with all my heart. When thoughts contrary to this wanted to enter my mind, I now knew they were not mine, and I didn't have to believe them. This broke a pattern in my belief system that brought tremendous freedom and truth to my identity. I was free to be the "daughter of the king" that I was designed to be. In essence, I could tell those "other" thoughts where to go!

Now my big challenge was to learn how to renew my mind. I had a lifetime of lies to unlearn and wrong thought patterns to untangle. In a very real way, I have had to learn how to think again. It wasn't easy and sometimes it still isn't. The enemy is always watching and ready to exploit our tiniest weakness or the slightest dropping of our guard in order to secure a foothold and gain an advantage.

By attributing my impure thoughts to an unclean spirit, I am not in any way trying to "pass the buck" or to excuse my sin. Eve was deceived into sin, but was still accountable to God for her actions. An unclean spirit may have spoken to me, but I chose to listen, I chose to agree, and I chose to follow. I still had to confess my sin to God, repent of it, and receive forgiveness and cleansing.

Being delivered from that unclean spirit did not mean that I would never have to worry about my thought life again. It meant that I did not have to live in bondage to my impure thoughts. My sinful nature is corrupt enough on its own to get me in trouble even without an unclean spirit. I still have to make the day-by-day and moment-by-moment decision for purity rather than impurity, to listen to God's Spirit instead of to the enemy.

Not all of our impure thoughts or illicit fantasies are necessarily the result of an unclean spirit in our lives. Sometimes they are simply the product of our own extremely creative sinful mind and nature. The point is this: if we struggle with impure thoughts (and we all do to one extent or another), we need to understand that this is *not* what God intended and we *don't* have to give in and accept it. We *don't* have to live in bondage. We *don't* have to live in desperation, quiet or otherwise. We can be *free*.

Four years ago, when all this began, I did not understand these things. I did not even understand how or why I had made such a colossal mistake. I felt remorse for what I had done because I knew in my heart that it was wrong, but I was not truly repentant. Not at first, anyway, not even after I confessed to Bob. In the beginning I did not comprehend the magnitude of my sin enough to be repentant. My self-deception and self-delusion were such that part of me wanted to continue the adulterous relationship even as the rest of me wanted to get out of it and set things right again. I knew I was wrong, but I really had no clue just how *terribly* wrong I was.

At the time, I was a "desperate housewife" and didn't even know it. I was busy yet bored. It wasn't anything Bob had done or had not done. Even in the midst of my sin I loved Bob deeply and was deeply committed to our marriage and family. My self-deception and self-delusion was such that I thought I could have all of that and still have this other relationship as well.

*I recognized that being dishonest with my feelings was a sin.*

The pattern of my life since childhood had been to do everything I could to make other people happy, whether it was my parents or Bob or my children—whoever. I grew up in a home where there was very little shouting. I learned early on to "stuff" my feelings rather than express them honestly (which might have involved shouting), and I deluded myself into believing that this was the "Christian" or "spiritually mature" way to deal with my emotions. I avoided confrontation like the plague! Bob isn't afraid of his own negative feelings like I am. So when he expressed his anger and vocalized frustration about anything, I found myself shutting down. I would suppress my honest feelings and my desire to talk back and feel spiritually superior to him because I was "in control" when he wasn't. Meanwhile, Bob was just being honest and participating in some healthy venting. Here I thought I was being so mature, but in actuality, it was Bob who was living in honesty and truth!

## A Desperate Housewife

I lived in this state of delusion and repressed emotions for years, never realizing that what I thought was emotional and spiritual maturity on my part was really an emotional pressure cooker slowly building to the breaking point. It was only in the aftermath of adultery and during the long and painful healing process that I gradually and finally came to understand what I had been doing to myself emotionally all those years. I also recognized that being dishonest with my feelings was a sin. In many cases I lived a life of denial, not living according to truth. I thought I was being good when really I was being untruthful and dishonest. It was my counselor and dear friend in Phoenix, Dr. Lois Burkett, who broke my paradigm that anger was a sin.

I never "exploded" emotionaliy. When my breaking point came, it was so subtle that I was not even aware of it. A man entered our lives whom Bob and I were trying to help. He took an immediate interest in me, lavishing me with praise and attention and expressions of appreciation whenever he could. I wasn't emotionally ready for such a continual barrage of affection and affirmation, even though I thought I was.

At first I did not respond outwardly to his efforts to get close to me. I thought it was "cute" that he was so interested in me, but I *knew* that nothing was going to come of it. I was too strong in the Lord, too mature in my faith. My love for Bob and for my children would never allow anything to intervene that would jeopardize those relationships. I was "in control." At the same time, deep within, I felt flattered and genuinely pleased at the attention. Subtly, and below my conscious awareness, my emotionally repressed self began to feed on his compliments and affirmation. It quickly became almost an addiction. The more I received, the more I wanted, and emotional seeds were planted that soon sprouted, grew, and eventually bore the bitter fruit of adultery.

*Feelings are real, but they are most often not true.*

Another girl came into the picture. Faced with the sudden threat of "losing" him, jealousy flared up in my heart. That is when I lost control. I became desperate, doing whatever I had to do to shift his attention back to me, even responding more openly to him than I had before. I didn't *really* want him (so I thought), but I loved the fact that he wanted *me* so badly. That which I thought I controlled now controlled me. From that point on, it was only a matter of time before our relationship became physical and sexual.

In the middle of it all, I thought I could have my cake and eat it too. I thought I could have a great marriage and a happy family and still have this other guy who adored me. Can I do this and not get caught? How long will this last? Looking back on it now, I shake my head in disgust that I could ever have thought such stupid things, but that's how deceived I was at the time—how self-deluded I had become. All I was doing was feeding my selfish desires.

Although deep in my heart I knew I was wrong, I wasn't afraid of consequences. I thought I was invincible. The whole affair gave me a sense of exhilaration. I can do this! It made me feel very alive.

That just goes to show how unreliable our feelings can be! Emotions are fickle and highly deceiving. We can *feel* so much "in love" when all we are doing is responding to a chemical release in our bodies. That's how it was with me.

At the height of it all, I was too self-deceived to recognize the signs that should have told me that all of it was wrong and could not possibly last. Feelings are real, but they are most often not true.

All in all, the affair was rather short. From the time it first got sexual to the time I confessed to Bob was about three weeks. At first I felt great, but gradually I progressed to an inner torment. I wrestled with my conscience because I knew better. Sometimes it was as though there were two Audreys: the one who knew better, and the one who wanted to continue in sinful self-indulgence. *What are you doing, Audrey? You know this is wrong!* I don't care...it's fun! *But now you're having to lie to your husband and your kids!* What they don't know won't hurt them! *Audrey, you're messing everything up! This is stupid!* Maybe so, but I'm loving all this attention. *Audrey, you know this can't last. You're setting yourself up for disaster.* I'll deal with that when the time comes.

At that time, I really didn't understand the consequences that would follow. My life up to then had been essentially carefree and happy-go-lucky. I had never faced anything like this before, and it was not until my relationship with this other man got physical that my eyes began to open. I knew it had to end.

Because he was single and unattached, we mutually agreed that he would leave town. It took him a couple of weeks to pull everything together. As an indicator of just how strong the bond(age) still was between us, we continued to see each other during that time when he was preparing to leave, and several of those meetings became sexual. Finally, he left town.

How could this have happened? I was a "desperate housewife" and didn't know it! It didn't begin to dawn on me how desperate I was until I did something *shocking*—and totally unexpected—without notice; something that I never dreamed I would ever or could ever do.

A couple of days after the "other man" left town, I confessed the whole thing to Bob. Bob called Leo. Leo made sure that Bob and I stayed together that night and that I confessed to my parents. Leo also knew that Bob and I needed not to be alone in facing this crisis. That's how Bob and I ended up on an airplane to Phoenix, Arizona.

At the time Bob and I left for Phoenix, no one at home (other than my parents) suspected a thing. We have always been spontaneous and had a love for adventure, so this was just another stint in the lives of Bob and Audrey. Little did they know that we were dying from pain and grabbing at any glimmer of hope.

The plane ride was continued torture. We couldn't begin to express our hurt to each other, so we just sat there, inches away from each other physically, but miles apart emotionally. At one point I happened to glance down and noticed that Bob had taken off his wedding ring. Tears streamed down my face. I began to wonder whether I had committed the unforgivable sin. Even though Bob was making steps to stay, I knew he wanted to run.

We flew from Winnipeg to Toronto, where we had an all-night layover. The seats in the airport waiting area were molded to accommodate people who were actually sitting, so lying down was extremely uncomfortable. Nevertheless, I managed to get somewhat comfortable, using my purse as a pillow. Bob sat in the row across from me and stared at me. I couldn't even begin to imagine what he was thinking or feeling. All I knew was that I felt condemned and doomed. Bob sat there all night writing on his handheld organizer.

That night Audrey and I spent in the Toronto airport was probably the longest night of my life. As I sat there, watching her, my mind was so conflicted. I loved her. I wanted her to be comfortable. But the questions! The pain! The sense of grief and irretrievable loss! The confusion! But mostly, the anger that swept over me like a wave then receded, only to return and wash over me again with the same intensity as before.

During that horrible flight from Winnipeg to Phoenix, I took off my wedding band, again looking for a reaction that would affirm to me in some way that she loved me. I was angry, sure, but mostly I was confused. The whole thing was completely unfathomable to me. How could this have happened? Audrey and I didn't have problems like this! That was the biggest thing. I couldn't get beyond it. *Audrey, how could you have been so dumb? So stupid? And now you say you love me?* It just didn't wash.

Journaling on my organizer at the airport that night was therapy for me. I needed to get some of my thoughts on "paper," so to speak, because I was not in any state to say them to Audrey directly. In one of my entries I wrote:

> You say, "I love you," and how I wish and pray I could believe that with all my heart. What hurts the

most is that you chose not to love but to give what was ours and made a choice to love another. Now that that's over, *I feel like a spare tire or a fifth wheel being used for an emergency.*

When will the pain and doubt subside? I don't know, but soon, I hope. When all the pain and doubts subside, I don't know what's going to happen. How does something so ugly and sinful happen to someone as beautiful and righteous as you? I still see what took place as so unbelievable; maybe this is where the problem lies. For me, reality is hard to face—I can only imagine how difficult it is for you.

Audrey, I'm sorry. Though I was there, you didn't come to me, and you rebelled against God. I know His love is unconditional, and it's being expressed to both you and me. Oh, how I pray for His love to be expressed through me for you. Audrey, my wife, I love you.

Leo's assistant picked us up at the airport. Bless his heart, he was such a happy and outgoing guy, while Audrey and I were dying inside. Our destination was a beautiful resort in Phoenix, courtesy of Leo's Sunday school class. In spite of all the beauty and luxury surrounding us, the one thing on our minds was seeing Leo. Audrey and I were like two drowning people in a lake, and Leo was our life preserver. At that moment, it seemed that he was the one connection we had together. We hoped desperately that he could say or do something that would start to build the bridge between us and make things all right again.

As it turned out, because of his conference responsibilities, Leo was not able to see us until midnight. He came to our room at the resort and began to ask pointed questions in his blunt, New York style. Leo's questions, though challenging, were not accusing. He started off by questioning Audrey about her rebellion.

Rebellion! I certainly didn't feel rebellious! I still felt like my old self: sweet, teachable, and giving. I loved Bob without question; I just enjoyed the attention of someone else too. How ludicrous that attitude appears to me now! Of course, my adultery was the epitome of rebellion! Deception is a powerful mind-bender. It helps us justify and encompass sin as part of our already existing life. It brings no warning of pain or devastation, but promises us that sin will add to our life without taking anything away.

> *We hoped desperately that he could say or do something that would start to build the bridge between us.*

Leo told me that *all* women are naturally rebellious; it's a biblical truth. Eve rebelled against God in the Garden of Eden. As a result, God pronounced a two-fold curse on Eve: first, she would have pain and sorrow in childbirth, and second, her desire would be for her husband, but he would rule over her. This was not sexual desire, but the desire to usurp authority. Part of the curse on a woman is that she has both sides of her brain working simultaneously, while men work primarily with one side. A woman tends to think that she is smarter and wiser than her husband and wants to usurp his authority, even though God has placed her husband in the position of leadership. It is an attitude of rebellion.

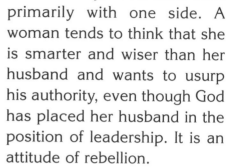

*That which seemed so right at the time turned out to be so wrong!*

I was just beginning to process the rebellion issue when Leo hit me with his next question: "When did you begin to disrespect Bob?"

That was another shocker! During our seventeen years of marriage, I had always made the deliberate choice to respect Bob. I had refused to talk against him to others, to complain about him, or ever to talk him down. Yet, again, I had to acknowledge that my adultery showed utter disrespect for Bob. I realized then that I was not yet at the place where I could face the full reality of what I had done, but I promised Leo that I would pray and seek God as to when I had begun to disrespect Bob in my heart.

I was a desperate housewife who went looking for love in the wrong place, even though there was plenty of love right there in my own home among my own family. That which seemed so right at the time turned out to be so wrong! That which felt so good for a moment opened the door to years of pain, heartache, anguish, and regret. My naïve and presumptuous confidence in my own spiritual maturity and in the invincible strength of my marriage were stripped away to reveal the rottenness of rebellion and disrespect at the core.

And that was just on the first night! What would the rest of the week bring?

## Endnotes

1. Cited on http://www.manhaters.com/p_catchacheaterstats.asp

2. NCPCE Online, "Current Statistics," http://www.nationalcoalition.org, cited in ibid.

3. Ibid.

4. Ibid.

5. Ibid.

6. *USA Today*, Dec. 21, 1998, cited in ibid.

7. *Washington Post*, March 30, 1999, cited in ibid.

8. Maggie Scarf, *Intimate Partners* (New York: Random House, 1987, reissued 1996 by Ballentine), cited in ibid.

9. Cited in ibid.

# Chapter Three

# *Covered*

Our first night in Phoenix with Leo was a real eye-opener for both of us. No sooner did he have Audrey contemplating the reality of her rebellion and disrespect than he turned to me and let me have it: "Bob, you're lazy!"

"What do you mean?" I protested. "I'm a busy man. I've always got lots of things going on."

"You're spiritually lazy. It's a natural tendency all men have. If all women are naturally rebellious, all men are naturally lazy. Again, it goes back to the Garden of Eden. Even as God placed a two-fold curse on the woman—pain and sorrow in childbearing and the desire to rule over her husband even as he rules over her—He also placed a curse on the man: *'Cursed is the ground for your sake; in toil you shall eat of it all the days of your life. Both thorns and thistles it shall bring forth for you, and you shall eat the herb of the field. In the sweat of your face you shall eat bread till you return to the ground, for out of it you were taken; for dust you are, and to dust you shall return'"* (Genesis 3:17b-19).

In other words, caring for the Garden was joy for Adam, but outside the Garden, raising crops for food would be toil involving constant labor and a lot of sweat and hard work. Man's natural tendency is to prefer the ease of life in the Garden over the life of toil in the world. Hence, fallen, sinful men tend toward laziness.

*If all women are naturally rebellious, all men are naturally lazy.*

Leo explained that when we are born of our mother, we are born into the natural, but when we are born again by the Spirit of God, we are born into the supernatural. A wise man recognizes and comes against the curse of the natural in order to rise above it and become supernatural. A Christ-like man understands that his ability to work is also his opportunity to exhibit Christ-likeness by sacrificing his life and time to provide for his family and advance the Kingdom of God.

In the same way, a Christ-like woman recognizes that when she submits to her husband, even against some of her own inclinations, she is responding to something supernatural that God is working out in her in which she operates not in rebellion, but in honoring what God has established in terms of leadership. She rises above her natural tendency to think she is smarter than her husband. It's not a matter of intelligence. Women are not smarter than men; they are simply more observant. Women receive more stimuli and thus are usually much better at multi-tasking than men are. Most men can do only one thing at a time and do it well.

The danger we face is in allowing Satan to deceive us into falling back into our natural tendencies: rebellion for women and spiritual laziness for men. Who knows what might have happened in the Garden if Adam had not been spiritually lazy? According to Genesis 3:6, when Eve was deceived by the serpent and took and ate the forbidden fruit, Adam was right there with her. Apparently, however, he made no attempt to intervene or to stop her from disobeying God. He was spiritually lazy. Instead of *covering* and *protecting* Eve during her time of deception and temptation, Adam not only said nothing, but, when given the chance, ate the forbidden fruit freely and with his eyes wide open!

> *Husbands who are spiritually lazy neglect to cover and protect their wives and their children.*

Husbands who are spiritually lazy neglect to *cover* and *protect* their wives and children. They lay their marriages and families wide open to spiritual attack and make them vulnerable to the enemy's lies. This is the truth that I had to face that first night in Phoenix, and it was a bitter pill to swallow because it stung my pride. After all, *I* was the wronged victim here! Audrey had betrayed *me*; I had not betrayed her. She had been unfaithful to *me*; I had not been unfaithful to her. I had *always* been the dutiful, faithful, loving husband (at least in my own mind) and then she had done this to me! Although I wasn't fully ready then to receive it, that first night in Phoenix I had to start dealing with the reality that I, in fact, had *not* been fully the husband I should have been. Without a doubt, Audrey was accountable to God for her actions, but I had to acknowledge the unpleasant truth that my lack of spiritual diligence with regard to my family—my spiritual laziness—had also contributed to what happened. Had I understood and practiced the principle of *covering* my wife and family, the adultery might never have occurred.

This understanding didn't happen instantly on our first night with Leo, not at all. I wanted to be angry. I deserved to be angry. Rather, it was a process of revelation and exchange. I spent time alone in God's presence; He turned on the light and loved me away from myself. Please understand, I wasn't being condemned in His presence; He was loving me. The great revelation was not my participation with sin, but rather His abundance of love, mercy, and grace being extended to me. That was the great exchange: me surrendering my inability for His grace.

It was my lack of understanding of the *covering* principle that also caused me at first to want to tell everybody what Audrey had done and to declare my innocence, making her the villain and me the hero. Leo had recognized that danger right away and immediately cut it off, reminding me of Proverbs 25:2 that says, *"It is the glory of God to conceal a matter."* God's desire for our situation was healing and restoration, which called for, first of all, *concealing* or *covering* it for protection.

Every woman has a deep down desire to be covered; it is part of her God-designed makeup. Every man is designed by God to be a *coverer*, a protector of his wife and children. Part of the man's function is to be a buffer between his family and the harshness of the world.

This principle of covering relates also to one of the hot and controversial issues in today's society: women's submission to men. The Bible plainly teaches the submission of wives and the headship of husbands. Old Testament Jewish society was clearly patriarchal in nature. In the New Testament, the apostles Paul and Peter both deal with the subject of submission.[1] The key questions are "Who submits to whom?" and "What does it mean to be in submission?"

> *Submission has nothing to do with a man's "right" to "rule" over his wife.*

God never intended women *in general* to be in submission to men *in general*. That is one of the points where a great deal of confusion and misunderstanding exist today. God's purpose was for *a* woman to be in submission to *a* man, such as a daughter submitting to her father while she lives at home or a wife submitting to her husband. In both cases, submission does *not* mean being under a man's dictatorial rule (whether father or husband), but under his protection and cover. Submission has nothing to do with a man's "right" to "rule" over his wife, but it has everything to do with his privilege and responsibility to protect and to cover her.

Such submission cannot be coerced; it must first be *deserved*, and then *freely given*. When husbands are diligent in doing their part, which is to *"love your wives, just as*

*Christ also loved the church and gave Himself for her"* (Ephesians 5:25), they will find their wives willing to submit to the leadership, protection, and covering of such a man.

Concealing or covering the matter meant also that knowledge of Audrey's adulterous affair and its aftermath was to be kept on a strictly need-to-know basis. No one should know about it who did not *need* to know, and that included our children. Too often, parents in crisis make the mistake of trying to soothe their own pain and fear by sharing the crisis with their children when their children are not emotionally mature enough to deal with it. All that does is spread the misery and stoke the flame, and all of a sudden the whole situation becomes a lot worse. When we as parents are going through a rough time, whether adultery or some other relationship problem, we need to be transparent and vulnerable in dealing with the situation, but also careful in setting boundaries so that our children do not end up becoming unwilling consolers in something they have no business being a part of. No child wants to have to choose between Mommy or Daddy. It's not fair and it's not right to put them in the middle.

Concealing a matter is a sign of maturity in a marriage. The Bible says that a man will leave his father and mother and "cleave" (cling) to his wife and the two of them will become one flesh. It is vitally important for a husband and wife to be mature enough when they marry that they don't carry their problems back to their parents or to their children, but to the Lord. If they need outside help, they should turn to a neutral outsider, a pastor or some other trusted person who can give them biblical and godly counsel.

That same night, Leo talked about the story of the adulterous woman being brought to Jesus and how Jesus silenced her accusers with the words, *"He who is without sin among you, let him throw a stone at her first"* (John 8:7). Under Jewish law, the penalty for adultery was death by stoning, a very public execution that would be preceded by a very public humiliation—the ancient Middle Eastern parallel to Hester Prynne's scarlet "A." Jesus' simple statement, by turning the thoughts of the woman's accusers back upon themselves, concealed the matter because none of them now would dare pick up a stone and by so doing claim to be sinless. Jesus "clamped the lid" on it, so to speak, and the woman, rather than being subjected to public humiliation and death, found forgiveness instead.

The point of the story was pretty clear: I faced a choice. On the one hand, I could choose the route of the woman's accusers and broadcast Audrey's sin all around, subjecting her to public shame and approbation while satisfying my own bruised, selfish pride and offended self-righteousness. On the other hand, I could choose the route Jesus had taken and I could *cover* Audrey's offense so that she would be protected and could experience forgiveness and restoration.

Conflict raged in my mind between doing what was *right* and doing what I *wanted* to do. As Audrey's husband, and as a follower of Christ, I knew that the *right* thing to do was to conceal and cover. At that time, however, my pain was still so raw and my wound so livid that a big part of me wanted to strike back and hurt Audrey as much as she had hurt me. Control with the hidden intent to punish.

This illustrates why getting solid, biblical counsel *immediately* in a crisis is so important. This soon after the blowup, neither Audrey nor I were able to think clearly enough to make the right decisions on our own. Without Leo's firm but compassionate guidance during that critical time, I don't know what I would have done. Our story may have had a very different and far more tragic outcome.

*Getting solid, biblical counsel immediately in a crisis is so important.*

Another thing Leo stressed that first night was that Audrey and I *pray* together every day, without fail. Prayer is one of the most powerful weapons for covering that we have in our spiritual arsenal. In America, the divorce rate is approximately one out of every two couples, even among couples who attend church regularly. According to a Gallup poll, for Christian couples who pray together daily, the divorce rate drops to one out of every 1,152! Leo told us that out of 10,000 couples he had counseled, he had never met a couple that prayed together daily that had gotten a divorce.

Leo was very forceful about our praying, which is what we needed at the time. He said, "Before you go to bed tonight, you *will* get on your knees, you *will* gaze into each other's eyes, and you *will* pray together." Looking into each other's eyes while we prayed was very important because the eyes are the windows of the soul. There is greatly heightened intimacy between people who look at, connect with, and touch each other as they pray. In other words, the person we are most intimate with is the person we pray with the most! That's why it is dangerous for us to pray more with a prayer partner than with our spouse.

Believe it or not, but pornography is a counterfeit to prayer because it attempts to seize the imagination of someone who is ultimately creative. When a husband and wife do not pray together, they do not have a sufficient outlet for their God-given creativity, which then becomes more prone to being captured by the allurements of the world.

That first night in Phoenix, prayer was the *last* thing I wanted to do! Four years later, however, I can say that what sustains us today is the prayer life that Audrey and I share. Whenever crisis comes in a marriage, prayer is usually the first thing to go, and yet it is the most important thing to maintain.

Despite my feelings, Audrey and I did pray that night. There was a lot of crying, some hand-holding, and a kiss, but we looked into each other's eyes and prayed. It was little more than "God, we need You," which was all we could muster at the moment, but we were face to face, eye to eye, breath to breath.

We even danced together that night. There was a song on the radio that talked about sexual healing. Boy, did we ever need a lot of that! And that was exactly what God had in mind. His rescue plan was in place, and although we were still in the dark about many things, God could see it all from His perspective. We made it through our second night together, our second night after Audrey had dropped her bombshell in the office that Tuesday.

The next morning, we were in the car with Leo, and a selected worship song was playing. Audrey and I just sat there, and I stared out the window, crying. After several minutes, Leo turned the music down and said, "I just needed to know whether you had breakthrough last night."

We did. Our healing had begun, but we still had a long, long way to go.

⊹═══⊹

As the week wore on, we met a few more times with Leo as his schedule permitted. Even after our breakthrough in prayer that first night, I was still wrestling constantly with my hurt, anger, and bitterness. It was a real struggle. For the longest time, I could not understand why Leo always seemed to single me out. To my mind, he was letting Audrey off lightly, while lowering the boom on me. What was going on here? After all, Audrey was the one who strayed, not me.

One morning Audrey and I were sitting across the table from Leo in his office and he was counseling us—but it was always directed toward me. I sat there thinking, and finally spoke up, "Why are you always picking on me? She's the one with the problem! I want to see some action over here!" I just didn't get it.

Leo knew what I was struggling with. He said to me, "You profess to be spiritual, and the innocent one in all of this. Well, let's test that. Let's see how spiritual you really are. You keep saying Audrey was deceived. Are you going to base your relationship now on the strength of deception or on the strength of spiritual character? First Corinthians 11:3 says that God is the head of Christ, Christ is the head of the man, and the man is the head of the woman. Ephesians 5:25-27 says that husbands are to love their wives as Christ loves the Church and gave Himself for her in order to sanctify her and cleanse her and present her glorious and holy, without spot, wrinkle, or blemish."

His point was that a Christian husband is responsible before God for the countenance of his wife. He is not responsible for her actions or her choices, because each person must give an accounting of himself or herself before God (Romans 14:12), but his leadership and his actions will be reflected in her countenance. On the surface, it may seem unfair that someone else's spiritual condition or happiness may be shaped or in some way dependent on our actions, but that is part of the reality of accepting our God-given role of leadership in the home.

> *A Christian husband is responsible before God for the countenance of his wife.*

Leo leaned across the table, looked me squarely in the eye, and said, "I need to know whether or not you will be the man of God to keep this home together. It's up to you. What Audrey did is in the past. What's done is done. What happens next depends on you."

Leo understood something that I could not yet see. In talking with Audrey, he knew that she was remorseful over what she had done. She was not yet fully repentant—her repentance came in layers over the weeks and months that followed as she became more and more spiritually sensitive—but she was remorseful. I was not. Leo knew that unless he could lead me to a higher spiritual level, I was in danger of embracing my bitterness and using it to justify my anger and my rejection of Audrey. That was one reason he was so straightforward and so brutally blunt with me; he had to shock me back to reality: *this is not all about you.* He had to jolt me into recognizing again my God-given role as the protector and coverer of my marriage and family.

I told Leo I *would* be the man of God I was supposed to be and would do everything in my power to keep our home and family together. It was the right and noble thing to say, but it wasn't easy. I viewed our marriage as a failure and more than that, myself. Everything was in question: our marriage, our past, and our future. I also sensed that it would not be easy to *do*. Many difficult challenges lay ahead for both Audrey and me, but I knew we both wanted a life together. Deep down, I knew she loved me, but closer to the surface, I wasn't ready to trust again. And I still had so many questions of why and how this all happened, while being crippled with the fear of it happening again.

When we first arrived in Phoenix, I was still hoping for an escape, a miracle prayer to take it all away. I wasn't ready to go back. I didn't want to face my job and my precious church family. How was I to survive, let alone everyone else who would learn about what was going on? I now knew running was not the answer. If we had done that, our marriage would not have survived.

As the week wore on, I really began to warm to Phoenix. It was a gorgeous city, and I found its palm trees and warm weather therapeutic. Add to that the wonderful pastor's conference, and I really felt quite safe while we were there. We still both had the enormous emotional trauma to work through, but our week in Phoenix was a life saver. We lived for every moment Leo could spend with us. Overall, it was not much, but he made good use of the time we did have with him. It was good just knowing that someone else knew, just knowing that we weren't alone. Instead of hiding or running away to lick our wounds, we were getting help, and wherever there is help, there is also *hope.*

Audrey and I walked together along the roads in Phoenix and enjoyed the beauty of the city and the climate. We picked oranges and even laughed a little. The strain between us was very obvious, however. The tension would lessen slightly, and then suddenly I would catch myself and remember what had happened. I know Audrey was hurt and disappointed because I wasn't ready to be okay yet. She has always been the more impetuous and upbeat of the two of us, and I think she was already impatient for things to improve. True to her background and experience up to this time, she wanted an instant healing, but I wasn't ready for that. As time went on, we both realized that an instant healing also was not God's highest and best plan for us. He wanted a deep healing and a thorough cleansing, and it would take a lot of dying to selfish desires on the part of both of us before that would come about. In the process, we would learn what *true* love really was.

*Wherever there is help, there is* hope.

One day late in the week of our visit to Phoenix, I was hit with my first panic attack. I had heard of panic attacks, but didn't really know what they were. Until I had one for myself, I don't think I really believed in them. All of a sudden, the thought occurred to me, *"What if Audrey's pregnant?"* I was sitting in one of the conference meetings at the time, and the thought rattled me so much that I had to get up and walk out. I was really starting to freak out. Fear washed over me in waves, my hands began to shake, I started gasping for breath, and for a little while I wasn't able to think very coherently.

Once the initial spasm of panic passed, I settled down a little and decided that I needed to get Leo's take on this latest wrinkle. I figured it would blow him away the same way it had me. I anticipated a reaction like, "Well, Bob, I don't know. I never considered that. Let me think about it and get back to you."

After the meeting, I found Audrey and Leo and together we walked toward the main church building. "I apologize for leaving the meeting early," I said to Leo, "but I had a sudden thought. What if Audrey's pregnant? What do we do then?"

Leo never missed a beat; his step never faltered. He simply said, "God's grace will be sufficient."

"That's it?" I nearly shouted. "That's your answer? God's grace will be sufficient? You're nuts!" I felt like punching him.

Cool and calm as ever, Leo said, "When the time comes, His grace *will* be sufficient."

I couldn't see it then, but I can say today with complete assurance that God's grace *is* sufficient. At that time I had only begun seeing beyond myself to realize what a delicate circumstance we were in. So much of what I'd always believed to be true was now being tested. Today Audrey and I have allowed grace to be perfected in our weakness and have come to know the love of our heavenly Father—as never before.

# Covered

Our week in Phoenix ended. We said goodbye to Leo, and Bob and I flew home to Winnipeg. We had made it! (So far.) One week after I had confessed to Bob the absolute worst thing I had ever done; one week after he learned how I had betrayed his trust and given to another man that which rightfully was Bob's alone; one week after the explosion into our lives of the revelation that has destroyed countless marriages; Bob and I were still together. That in itself was a miracle of God. He had poured out His love, mercy, and grace on us lavishly, and we needed all that we could get. Leo was part of the miracle. Thanks to his wise, compassionate, and godly counsel, we had been rescued. We were now on the road to recovery—barely—but we were not all right yet, not by a long shot.

The hope that filled our fragile hearts gave way at times to deep and dark despair. Desperately, we clung to the smallest thread of optimism, the tiniest fragment of a reason to believe that things would get better. I remember sitting down at the phone table in our resort room in Phoenix one day and praying with my head between my knees. I didn't just ask God to forgive me and help me, I *begged* Him. Even at this stage I still felt a very strong control from the other relationship. I asked God to take away the feelings I had for this other man and to break any kind of controlling spirit that was over me. Fierce battle raged in my mind and heart. I remembered the words of Gordon Lindsay: "If you are in desperate need of deliverance, do not hesitate to cry to the Lord. He hears those who call upon Him with all their heart."

One thing Leo had stressed to me was the importance of breaking off *all* contact with the other man: phone calls, emails, everything. Bob reinforced this by making me promise that I would have nothing more to do with this person. One might think that this was an obvious choice at this point—a "no-brainer"—but deception still had its crazy grip on me. I still wanted to imagine that I could mend my marriage and still be friends with the other man.

*If you have any hope or any desire to save your marriage, you must break off the adulterous relationship* immediately, deliberately, *and* completely.

My pattern had been to call a certain phone number and get a certain feeling. It was so selfish; sin always is. Everything was all about me. The months of healing and restoration that followed included a slow death to this selfish part of me. Early on, one of my biggest struggles was resisting the temptation—any temptation—to seek comfort from the wrong person. I emptied my house and office of any sign of him. Every reminder of him—every picture, every belonging of his, every gift he had given me, no matter how nice or expensive—went straight into the trash. It was harsh, and it was deliberate—and it was absolutely necessary. The hard shell of deception and sin had to break, and I had to make deliberate choices to work with God in softening my heart.

Many times since Bob and I have started counseling others, people in similar situations to ours have asked, "Do I really have to break completely my relationship with this person?" In some cases they were having an affair with their best friend.

Our answer: *Absolutely!* If you have any hope or any desire to save your marriage, you must break off the adulterous relationship *immediately, deliberately,* and *completely.* There is abundant evidence to the fact that once a relationship becomes sexual it will continue to be sexual as long as the people continue to see each other. Once that step has been taken, it is almost impossible to turn back.

This was true in my case. As soon as my relationship with this other man became sexual, I knew it had to end. Even so, during the three weeks that elapsed before he left town, we continued to see each other, and we had sex on several occasions. A big part of me wanted this relationship to continue because I falsely believed it was meeting a need in my life. Only a radical and complete break with him and permanent physical separation brought it to an end. I am quite certain that had we continued to see each other, the sexual conduct would have continued to the eventual destruction of my marriage.

Sin is not something to play around with. Sin is a cancer that must not be coddled or ignored. And, like a physical cancer, sin will kill if it is allowed to run its course. James 1:14-15 says, *"Each one is tempted when he is drawn away by his own desires and enticed. Then, when desire has conceived, it gives birth to sin; and sin, when it is full-grown, brings forth death."*

Sin has to be cut out at the source like emergency radical surgery. It doesn't matter how close the two of you might have been before it got sexual; you've got to get free and get free *now*. Don't open yourself up to any further attack by the enemy. As Leo would say, "Whatever is a tool of the enemy is a tool of the enemy! Stop! Break that contact *now*! You can't reestablish covenant as long as you continue to embrace that which is attacking the covenant!"

I've always been a pretty determined person. I know what I want and how to get it. From a fairly young age I gained a reputation as the "Can Do Kid." Whenever something needed to be done, even if I had never done it before, I would say, "I can do that," and then I would do it. For the first seventeen years of my marriage I lived almost constantly in "performance mode" and wasn't even aware of it. It took having to face something that I could *not* handle to help me see how truly helpless and dependent I was.

By the time we got back from Phoenix, the shock of everything was beginning to wear off some and my own drive kicked in. The "Can Do Kid" was at it again. I wanted to do everything possible to earn Bob's forgiveness, to make him love me again, and to re-ignite all the loving feelings I had for him. I took it on like a project. Do you see the fallacy here? *I* wanted to do all these things. After all, I was the one who had always been "in control." Only now things were different. I still did not fully understand that I was now in a situation that was *beyond* me, but I was about to find out.

Valentine's Day came just a few days after Bob and I got back from Phoenix. To say I overdid it would be an understatement! I had heart balloons, stickers, presents, and treasure hunts ready for him throughout the day. But all the calculated determination and "worked-up" romance in the world could never compare to the warmth of love that is free from "trying" and secure in trusting. Bob and I were not at that place, and I wondered if we ever would be again. At any rate, nothing could have prepared us for what happened next.

Six weeks had passed since my affair had first become sexual; three since it had ended and I had confessed to Bob. I felt like I'd been through enough hardship for a lifetime. I was weary, empty, and fighting to face the future when a new dynamic came into the picture. My monthly cycle was late. I knew I couldn't be pregnant, so I didn't bother Bob with the information.

*All the calculated determination and "worked-up" romance in the world can never compare to the warmth of love that is free from "trying" and secure in "trusting."*

A few more days went by and I knew that my period was not just late; I had missed it entirely. I finally told Bob, and we bought a drugstore pregnancy kit. The result was unclear, so we bought another one. Same result. I continually reassured myself that there was no chance at all that I was actually pregnant. After another pregnancy test and an actual trip to the walk-in clinic, we both sat in the doctor's office when he informed us of the news.

"The test came back positive. Do you want to continue the pregnancy?" All in the same breath.

God is so merciful. Unknown to me at the time, He was already preparing me to deal with the news. That very morning, for the first time since my adultery, I had read the biblical story of David and Bathsheba. As never before I had felt the heartbreak that both David and God went through. It wasn't until David took innocent blood, however, that God actually verbalized how displeased He was. David's cover-up cost him more in his relationship with God than did his first sinful act of adultery. After reading that story, I made up my mind at that moment that if I was indeed pregnant, that baby was an innocent life, and two wrongs would not make a right.

I found it ironic that the doctor gave us the option so quickly. Perhaps he sensed our devastation. As we walked out of the doctor's office, Bob locked his elbow around mine. My knees buckled. I looked into Bob's eyes. We were both scared and speechless. I felt Bob's pain at that moment, but for the first time in weeks, I also felt his strength. Every bit of strength I could muster up to face this new reality was not enough. I was completely spent. After I committed adultery and confessed, I didn't think I could face the future. With this new reality—a baby on the way—I didn't think I could face life.

From the day we were married, Bob and I had always dreamed of having children, and in time, God blessed us with three of them. Christopher Robert Meisner was first, arriving on October 31, 1986—"Hallelujah Day"! At nine pounds, eight ounces, he was big, beautiful, and perfect. In the days following his birth, I discovered my purpose for being. I loved *everything* about being a mom.

Janelle Audrey Meisner was next, born on May 8, 1989, weighing in at over nine pounds. She had dark hair and captivating blue eyes. Janelle was a special joy for us. Both Bob and I have all brothers for siblings, and we had pretty much resigned ourselves to the fact that our children also would probably all be boys. Janelle was such a wonderful surprise! We thanked God for blessing us with such a beautiful girl.

Finally, on October 25, 1991, our third precious baby was born: David Lee Meisner. Kids didn't get much cuter than this one. He is still cute, and probably always will be. David has always been my favorite boy's name, and it was reserved for him, a man after God's own heart.

One common characteristic of all three pregnancies was the sickness and nausea that I endured. With Christopher, for the first eight months I threw up every day, usually many times a day. With Janelle it was even worse. On average, I threw up twenty times a day and at one point ended up in the hospital with dehydration. It was more of the same with David, except that there were also two small children running around the house. Nonetheless, everything I went through, every bout of nausea, every discomfort was worth it to bring these three wonderful children into the world. It was just as Jesus said, *"A woman, when she is in labor, has sorrow because her hour has come; but as soon as she has given birth to the child, she no longer remembers the anguish, for joy that a human being has been born into the world"* (John 16:21).

Ten years later, a new reality stared us in the face. The law of genetics guaranteed that this baby would look different from the other three. Just a few weeks before, I had had to face my sin and announce it to my husband and parents. Now, I had to face my sin and announce it to the world. I had always desired to leave a legacy for the generations to come. With an emotional jolt I realized that no matter what else I did in this world, I would probably be remembered for the one big thing I did wrong. Never had I felt more vulnerable or more in need of Bob's support. The "Can Do Kid" was not so self-sufficient after all. If ever I felt like I couldn't do something alone, this was it.

> *I realized that no matter what else I did in this world, I would probably be remembered for the one big thing I did wrong.*

Suddenly, everything changed. Gone was our goal of trying to keep ourselves together and get through the pain without hurting others. Questions jumped into our heads like popcorn: How do we quit the church? Who do we tell? Where do we go? What do we do with the baby once it's born? It would have been so easy to have an abortion. One day I made an anonymous phone call to find out what the procedure would be. The woman I spoke to said casually that the pregnancy was detected early enough to render ten simple pills and the baby would be gone. I cried and repented to God for even making the phone call.

Even after returning from Phoenix, we made frequent and necessary calls to Leo. His advice and counsel continued long-distance. After we learned that I was pregnant, Bob called Leo and said, "Audrey's pregnant. What do we do?"

Leo answered very quickly and easily, "There is a baby on your doorstep. What do you think you are supposed to do?"

By this time, Bob had already started seeking counsel from other leaders in addition to Leo. He wasn't completely ready to accept everything that Leo said without getting a "second opinion." This only added to the confusion because Bob got different advice from different people. Some said that we should give the baby up for adoption. Others even told us that abortion was a legitimate option. One thing they all agreed on, however, was that we would *never* be capable of loving this child as much as our other three.

In the end, we concluded that Leo's counsel was the soundest and the most trustworthy for us to follow. The last thing we needed was ten people telling us to go in ten directions at once.

When we told Leo what others had said about our not being able to love this child like the others, he said in his straightforward, pull-no-punches style, "That's ridiculous! That's a shame to the body of Christ! What if you woke up tomorrow morning and found a baby on your doorstep? Wouldn't you care for that child?"

Leo then directly challenged Bob. "You have a decision to make, Bob. Fatherlessness is the plague of this generation. You can either contribute to the fatherlessness, or you can choose (make a quality decision) to be conformed to the character of your Creator, who says, 'I am a Father to the fatherless.'"

It was an easy answer. It was the *right* answer, but not an easy one to live out during a nine-month pregnancy. Doing the right thing is not always easy. Fear is right there attempting to rule you with its lies of you living in lack for the life choices you make. Sometimes doing the right thing is the hardest choice of all. As time went on, and even in the midst of our pain, anger, fear, and confusion, Bob and I became clear on one thing: we were committed to our Lord and Savior Jesus Christ. We were willing to do everything necessary to stay together, to see this crisis through, and to allow God to work His miracle wonder.

> *Doing the right thing is not always easy. Fear is right there attempting to rule you with its lies.*

One leader from whom Bob sought counsel confessed to him that his wife had been caught up in soulical/emotional adultery with another man. This leader told Bob that he had resigned himself to the fact that his marriage would never again be a "10." He had settled for an "8" out of "10," tops. Bob's response was, "No way! Our marriage is going to be 10 out of 10 or nothing! God is either a redeemer or He isn't; He is either a restorer, or He isn't. I will not accept anything substandard in this, because that's not the way God works!"

By and large, our culture is too willing to settle for mediocrity or second-best, particularly when it comes to relationships. Whether it is because they are too tired of searching or because they are resigned to the "fact" that a "perfect" or "10 out of 10" relationship is beyond their reach, too many people settle for "just so" relationships. Early hopes fade and dreams die as people slowly awaken to the reality that joy, happiness, contentment, and success are more elusive than they thought and now they feel trapped. Life has not delivered what they expected and true love seems a distant dream because they are looking in the wrong places.

This disappointment in life and love is one of the major factors that feeds the quiet desperation that so characterizes our modern western culture.

*Dependence teaches us to allow God to work His will and His way in our lives.*

People want to be happy but don't know where to find it. All the things that they expected would bring it have failed to deliver. Convinced that it is not to be found in their current circumstances, they start looking outside those circumstances, even pursuing other relationships in hopes of finding what they seek. Sometimes they can't even identify what it is they seek. All they know is that something is missing.

All of this goes back to the whole deception of "lack." The enemy convinces us that we will never have fullness in our relationships or in any other area of life, so we resign ourselves to second-best. By doing so, we cheat ourselves out of the best that God has to offer and is ready to bring into our lives if we will only cast ourselves upon His mercy. It is the difference between *desperation* and *dependence*. Desperation leads us to do shocking things without notice. Dependence teaches us to allow God to work His will and His way in our lives. Therein lies the secret to rescue and restoration—the answer to the quiet desperation of our generation.

One of the things that Bob and I decided on early was that we needed to leave Winnipeg, at least for a while, and move to a more neutral location so we could rebuild our lives and our relationship and protect our children in a place where we were not so well known. The safe choice was Phoenix, the scene of our initial rescue. My parents were reluctant to see us go but understood our reasoning and supported us in the move.

Our children embraced the move with typical youthful excitement over something new. They saw the whole thing as a big adventure. Of course, they knew nothing as yet of the adultery or the baby. Bob and I wanted to carefully and lovingly prepare just the right environment for them before bringing them into the picture. That day would have to come soon, because the baby I was carrying was not going to get any smaller!

Life suddenly became a whirlwind for us. There was so much to do, and quickly. We had to sell our house, quit our church, and pack up our children and belongings and haul them off to a strange new city. Bob was an American citizen and our children therefore were Americans born abroad. I, however, was Canadian, so we faced the potential prospect of a lengthy delay in getting paperwork approved that would allow me to enter the United States as a permanent resident.

One of my vivid memories is getting our house ready to sell. We had priced it to sell quickly (we hoped) and the real estate agent gave us tips on what to polish or paint to get the house ready to show. We worked day and night for several days fixing things up. One day I was in the boys' bedroom moving big furniture and painting the walls. Suddenly I stopped to embrace the miracle: I hadn't thrown up once! I had spent the day inhaling paint fumes and moving a bunk bed, yet somehow felt no repercussions on my pregnant body. This was so different from all my other pregnancies! I didn't understand it, but I closed my eyes and thanked God for His grace.

Special moments like that, when they came, were all the more precious because of the guilt and anger issues that we were still wrestling with. Bob's anger still flared up at unexpected times. One day I walked in the bedroom to see him glaring at me with a look so intense it bordered on hatred. He had been reading my journals. Journaling had been a precious outlet of expression for me for years in which I poured out my deepest thoughts to God. Every feeling, every doubt, every prayer went onto those pages, along with every insight or answer from God that came to me during those intimate times with Him. Nothing was more personal to me than my journals, and I had always felt that my "secrets" were safe with Him.

Bob had discovered some of the passages where I described my feelings for the other man and my struggles with the whole relationship. I can't imagine how painful it must have been for him to read those things. Unfortunately, I responded with offended anger. My privacy had been violated. Ignoring his accusations, I simply gathered up all my journals, took them outside and threw them into the garbage. Later, when I mentioned the incident to Leo, he did not sympathize with me for one moment. Instead, he told me that under the circumstances I had no right to privacy, and that was that. Bob's trust had been shattered, and I was in no place to hide anything from him anymore.

*I just wanted life to be over. I felt as though I simply couldn't live another day.*

Another flare-up came on my birthday, two weeks after we learned I was pregnant. We had sold the house the previous weekend (an answered prayer!) and were staying at my parents' home so our house would remain perfect for viewing. I don't remember what triggered Bob's anger, but it was more severe that day than ever. He left the house in a rage, and I followed him in a light jacket. There was snow on the ground, and it was a particularly cold day. In all truth, it was the coldest day of my life, and I'm talking about more than just the weather. That was the day everything hit me: Bob's justified anger, a baby that I didn't know what to do with, and a future with everyone in the world finding out what had happened. I walked around trying to find Bob's car, but finally gave up. Plopping myself down into the snow on the side of the street, I put my head between my knees and sobbed. Bob found me eventually, but I didn't even want to get up. I just wanted life to be over. I felt as though I simply couldn't live another day. I was so numb that I didn't even feel the cold and I didn't care. I turned thirty-six years old that day.

As a mom, I really wanted to keep our kids safe from the situation for the moment, so I held myself together until times when I was alone or with someone I felt I could trust. One day I was with my dad in the parking lot of a nearby Home Depot when I broke down. I felt so horrible. I hated myself for what I had done, for the pain I had brought on Bob and on my parents, and the ruin that I feared I had brought on my family. Dad said something then that I will remember and cherish forever: "Audrey, this is something you did, but it's not who you are."

I can't describe what happened next. It was like surgery taking place in my soul, mending my identity, bringing truth to the lies that wanted to kill me, and applying God's perspective to my tortured spirit. And it all came from my own earthly father who cherished me and called me his own.

As we prepared to move, my friends couldn't support me emotionally because they had no idea what was really going on. I found this very difficult, because I wanted more than anything to pour my heart out to a couple of my closest girlfriends. Fear of making any more mistakes kept me from saying anything. Our church family had graciously released us, but wouldn't know until later the details of why we were leaving. We simply said, "This is something that we have to do." They brought food, helped us move, and hugged and kissed us good-bye.

In the end, crossing into the United States was easy. Before leaving Winnipeg we had checked with the emigration authorities. They needed to know how long we had been married and the citizenship status of our children. A process that normally took months took one week. We had to submit original documents to the consulate. We submitted them on a Friday, and they were returned approved on the following Friday!

We hit the border with four Americans and one Canadian. We showed them a list of the contents of our moving truck, paid a two-dollar fee, and we were across! Janelle and I flew to Phoenix from Minneapolis, while Bob and the boys drove the moving truck.

Such began our new life. We had no phone and no vehicle of our own. Bob's dad and his wife lived in Phoenix and had graciously consented to put us up for a few days until we found a place of our own. Janelle and I arrived on a Thursday; Bob and the boys pulled in on Saturday evening. The next morning, we borrowed the car and the five of us drove across town to Phoenix First Assembly. It was a huge church; Leo's Sunday school class alone was a couple hundred people. He knew we were coming and introduced us to the group. They welcomed us warmly and by the end of church that morning we knew we had some new friends.

This was the start of our "miracle week." That afternoon we bought a used mini-van that I had found with the help of Bob's dad. It was right in our price range, perfect for our needs...and a direct gift from God. The next morning, a real estate agent from our new church told us of a vacant house five minutes away from the church. The house had been sold, but the buyer had backed out at the last minute. The owners were willing to rent it to us on a month-by-month basis while they continued to try to sell it. This was another gift from God. Every rental home we had looked at required a one-year lease. There were too many unknowns in our lives at the moment to commit to that, so this was, again, perfect provision.

Paperwork took forty-eight hours. We had the truck on a seven-day rental, and it was due back by 6:00 on Wednesday. We got the keys to the house on Wednesday at noon and worked hard in hot weather for five hours unloading. Since we had no friends to call, three generations of Meisner men worked their muscles. It was close, but we made it. The truck was back at the rental agency by 6:00, and we went to church that night.

Everything about the past seven days spelled m-i-r-a-c-l-e! The house was beautiful and in a perfect location, and we had a vehicle to drive. As far as employment, Leo referred Bob to a television producer friend he knew in the southwest corner of Phoenix. It turned out to be a man I had known since I was a young girl. Ron Hembree and my dad were friends, and he was one of many guests who came to Winnipeg to appear on *It's A New Day*. Little did we know that he was also part of the miracle God had in mind to rescue us and to answer our prayers.

When Leo referred me to Ron Hembree, I didn't want to see him, not because of Ron, but because he was involved in Christian television, and I didn't want any more of that. He knew me and my father-in-law, and I just wanted to leave the past behind. Nevertheless, Leo and I went there for a pastors' breakfast. We were sitting in Ron's office and he asked, "What are *you* doing here?" I began to cry. Should I tell him? Yes! I told Ron my story. This big, strong, deep-voiced man started crying, too. He said, "Let's talk more after the meeting."

As we talked together, I learned that Ron had been through a terrible divorce himself, so he was very sensitive to my situation. Two days later I got a phone call. "Bob, how much money do you need to live?" Audrey and I had already discussed an amount, just in case Ron made an offer. I gave Ron the figure, and he said, "My wife Cathy and I prayed and discussed this and decided that if you asked for that very amount, we would hire you."

So, I went to work for Ron. I was still in such an emotional state, however, that all I did really was sit at a desk and stare at the wall in a daze. I couldn't put two thoughts together. Ron didn't have to hire me; he just did. He had been through a bad situation himself and in his huge compassionate heart he loved me. Nearly every day he checked on me. He put his strong hand on my shoulder and said, "You're going to be all right." I'm glad he believed it, because I didn't. I wasn't there yet.

I helped Ron produce his show, *Quick Study*, and the pay was enough for our family to live on. (He also provided family medical care for us and the birth of our baby, which was extremely generous.) But that wasn't all. Ron thrust me into ministry immediately. "There's an inner city ministry called Church on the Street that has a complete discipleship program with weekly morning Bible study. I'd like you to go once a week and teach it." I taught the class one time, but did not go back the next week. Ron confronted me. "Where were you this morning? Why weren't you at the class? That's a part of your job. I want you there every single week."

Ron gave me no choice in the matter. The discipleship course was full of beautiful people who had been on the street, in prison, and away from home; they were broken people, and I was one of them. Who was I, as broken as I was, to help them? That's how I felt at first. In the end, teaching that Bible study turned out to be the most rewarding time for me. It brought me tremendous healing. I literally preached myself back to life.

It was inevitable, of course, that we would tell our children what was going on, but we were thankful for the time we had to settle in to Phoenix, begin developing friendships, and reestablish ourselves as a family. Our biggest concern was *what* exactly we should tell them. Should we simply tell them that their mother was pregnant and simply wait to see what the baby looked like? Some people in our lives thought so. Audrey and I were in strong agreement, however, that we would tell them what they needed to know, and we both felt they needed to know that another person was involved. We didn't want them to one day feel betrayed because we hadn't shared the truth with them. Besides, we have always had a very open relationship with our kids.

Leo had talked to me about *covering* my wife and my children and our marriage. For so long I had been so obsessed with questions of "how" and "why" and a judgmental spirit toward Audrey that it was hard to think about anything else. Slowly, as I began to heal, I began to remember that as a husband and father, I had a God-given responsibility to be the priest, provider, and protector of my home. That is the essence of covering.

As the priest in the home, I am the one to go between my Father and my family. It means deliberately engaging myself in the activity of listening for the voice of God to give me His direction for our home, our marriage, and our children. My children are under my covering until the day they leave my home and make a home of their own and during that time I am responsible to God for *how* I cover them.

*I had a God-given responsibility to be the priest, provider, and protector of my home. That is the essence of covering.*

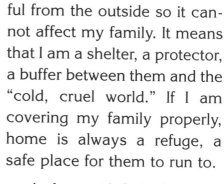

Covering means that I filter out anything harmful or hurtful from the outside so it cannot affect my family. It means that I am a shelter, a protector, a buffer between them and the "cold, cruel world." If I am covering my family properly, home is always a refuge, a safe place for them to run to.

As Leo said, fatherlessness is the plague of this generation. There are more fatherless homes today than ever before. In many cases, fathers are absent simply because they were never fathered themselves.

My own father was a great guy, but very quiet and communicative in his own way. As a young boy hungry for his father's approval, however, I was happy with anything he gave me. My dad had been my hero all my life. I admired and looked up to him. He was the leader, and I wanted to be just like him. Everybody liked my dad. He was strong, lovable, and happy. Though his words were few, he always had the right words for me. Just being around my dad would give me great feelings of confidence and security. I think that's what dads are for.

# Covered

The summer Audrey and I got engaged, Dad had called to inform me that he was leaving my mother after twenty-four years of marriage. I was crushed. Without knowing it, I closed off a compartment in my heart labeled "Dad" and kept it in reserve, hoping that he and Mom would get back together again. It never happened.

After nine years of marriage and finding myself quit stagnant and cynical in my Christian walk, I had an encounter with God, a vision in which He led me down a long corridor with doors on both sides. We stopped at one door that was dusty and covered with cobwebs. On the door was a rusted, gold-colored plate that said, "Father." I recognized it as the room I had reserved for my father. I knew this would be the end of our time together if we did not enter the room. We entered the room. The curtains were drawn, but there was a large throne there, and I heard my heavenly Father say, "This is the place for Me. With your deep love for your own father, you have shut Me out of your life." I repented, and gave Him the place on that throne in my heart. We began a fresh new relationship with me beginning to see God the Father as intimate and personal as Dad. The first words He spoke to me at that moment were words of *identity*. It is the *father* who imparts identity: *"This is My beloved Son, in whom I am well pleased"* (Matthew 3:17).

From that day, God began to father me and protect me and cover me. Injustice, ridicule, shame: God *never* does these things. But the enemy does, and why should I give place or participate in what the enemy wants to do to either my children or my wife? I should be their *covering*, their high tower, their place of refuge.

Covering has a lot to do with safety, healing, and discipline. (What responsible father does *not* give discipline?) Covering does *not* mean saying that everything is okay when it isn't, or ignoring and not addressing a problem or a sin. It *does* mean saying, "You're safe with me, and we're going to work this thing out."

> *Covering has a lot to do with safety, healing, and discipline. Covering does* **not** *mean saying that everything is okay when it isn't.*

We cover what we value. Right after Audrey's confession of adultery, I didn't value her. As a result, I wanted to expose her, I wanted to hurt her, I wanted to shame her, I wanted to punish her—all the very things the enemy wants to do. I didn't want to love and cherish her; I wanted to fix her. I thought that if I could make her feel bad enough about what she had done, I could secure our future and she would never do such a thing again.

Here's the challenge: how do you uncover someone's sin without uncovering her? That was Hosea's challenge. Hosea was a preacher of righteousness with a credibility problem: he was married to the town whore. People demand spiritual perfection from those behind the pulpit, which is nothing more than religiosity. This is the pedestal that Audrey and I were on that made our rescue and restoration such a ticklish and uncertain prospect.

As a husband, my challenge is to bring covering, healing, and wholeness to what sin has eroded and infected. My task is to create an environment that makes it attractive for Audrey to be faithful to me and to God. The way I do that is by making myself attractive to her in demeanor, spirit, and loving behavior. I do it by not being spiritually lazy but diligent about hearing and following the Lord and leading my family to do the same.

> *Husbands, as faithful followers of Christ, we set the pace. This is our role.*

When I was learning about covering, some of the instructions I received were, tell Audrey you love her and court her back. Forsake everything else. Break all other ties. Make it easy. Make your marriage so intriguing and challenging that there will be no hint of boredom and no reason to look elsewhere for satisfaction. Love conquers all.

Husbands, as faithful followers of Christ, we set the pace. This is our role. Somebody needs to be spiritual, and it had better be us. We are priests, providers, and protectors, and we are to provide a door of hope when all hope has flown. We are to provide new vision when vision has faded away. We are to stir up new dreams when old dreams have departed.

The problem is that too many men are lazy. Laziness is a huge part of the lives of many men. Guys, do you want to be romantic? Get a job. Provide for your wife. Put a sound financial plan together. Be strong and be consistent. Be an emotional support. In my covering, I am the one who has to be the strong one. I need to be a leader that my wife and children can trust, someone who brings emotional support, vision, hope, and safety. It's time to get spiritual.

Telling our children was a sober event, not that we were in mourning, but that we painstakingly went through each detail of how and when we would tell them. Bob and I knew this would be a defining moment in their lives. They would very likely adopt our perspective, so how we communicated the news was of utmost importance. If we told them this was a terrible thing, they would automatically shift into that paradigm. Yet, the sin *was* terrible! As always, our faithful God came through! He used Bob in a powerful way to demonstrate His character.

My mom was visiting us from Winnipeg. She knew what was going on and decided to walk and pray while we had our family meeting. Earlier, Bob had gone to one of the local department stores and bought three baby toys. The kids gathered upstairs in our bedroom and we all sat on the carpet. Bob had a huge blanket, and wrapped it over me like a tent. He then held me close to his chest.

"Kids," he said, "take a look at this picture. Whenever we make a mistake, and we go to our heavenly Father to ask forgiveness, He embraces us, holds us close, and covers us with His love just like I'm covering your mom." Bob then proceeded to tell the kids what I had done, and that I was now carrying a baby. I did not know ahead of time that he was going to cover me. I felt so loved and so cared for! The kids didn't have to see my face as Bob explained what happened. We knew they would have questions, and we offered to answer any of them. We comforted them by assuring them that we were completely committed to our marriage and that we had no plans of separation.

Afterwards, there was perfect peace in the room. Tears ran down our cheeks, and we all held each other. We knew this would bring us closer. The children embraced their new brother or sister with complete acceptance and excitement. Bob pulled out the three baby toys and said to the kids, "These are the first gifts that you will give to the baby." Certainly, our kids had feelings to deal with that only they could talk about, but God answered our prayers in keeping them all strong and secure.

Our family was intact, and it was *only* by the grace of God. We were *covered*!

### Endnote

1. Ephesians 5:21-33; Colossians 3:18; 1 Peter 3:1-6

# *Chosen*

A gift is not chosen; it is received. Our gift was chosen by the Giver of all good gifts, though not recognized as a gift at all. Yet, it was the greatest of all the gifts we'd ever received, even though it was produced among the most unlikely, and even the ugliest, of circumstances. This gift the enemy would have loved for us to disregard, for within it lay the depth of healing and the miracle of redemption. In times of rejection, God reminded His people, *"I have chosen you and will not throw you away. Don't be afraid, for I am with you. Do not be dismayed, for I am your God. I will strength-en you. I will help you. I will uphold you with my victorious right hand"* (Isaiah 41:9, 10, NLT). There was so much we still didn't understand.

Now that our children knew, it was time to tell some other people. Audrey and I both agreed that all of our broth-ers needed to know, as well as my parents. The first ones we told were my dad and his wife, Beth. I went to work, and Audrey made plans for a visit. Before coming over she warned them that she had something important to talk about.

We all sat down together and I spilled out our story; first, about the adultery, and then about the pregnancy and our firm decision to keep the baby. Neither Dad nor Beth offered a single word of condemnation or judgment. They were sobered by the pain we had already endured and wanted to support us in every way. Dad even thanked me for not aborting the baby and reassured us that this little one would be as much a grandchild as the others. Dad was the first member of Bob's family to know the truth. The mercy and love extended to me was overwhelming. I felt sobered and covered all at the same time.

As divorce survivors, Dad and Beth both said how thankful they were that Audrey and I were sticking together and were working things out in our marriage. As painful as our experience was for us, they said divorce was even worse. Dad said, "Had your mother and I had good counsel, we might have been together today. Knowing what we know now, Beth and I both wish we could have avoided the pain of divorce. We love each other very much and are happy together, but the toil, the pain, the heartache, and the ripping that takes place in a divorce are much more difficult than you could imagine."

During this whole time Dad was incredible. He never probed or asked questions. He had rolled with the punch when our family dropped everything and showed up on his doorstep on extremely short notice. He hadn't even known we were moving until two weeks before, but he and Beth graciously had opened their home to us. For all they knew, they might be stuck with our crazy family for months until we found work and a place of our own. But they had been willing to risk it, and Audrey and I would be forever grateful.

Unconditional love is the only way to describe the response we received from all the family members we confided in. With no exceptions, everyone was extremely forgiving—shocked, certainly!—but nonetheless loving. They each expressed thankfulness and appreciation for the fact that we were staying together, and they all pledged to do whatever they could to help. In many ways, it was quite a relief to share our story. I'm sure it must have answered a lot of questions, such as the reason for our sudden move and possibly even our weird behavior. It's impossible to put a price tag on the value of a family that loves and is willing to walk with you when we could have been so easily ostracized. Such a blessing is truly a gift from God and a priceless treasure.

We may have been rich in family, but we didn't have much when it came to money. Newly arrived from a foreign country, we soon discovered that even though Bob was an American, because he had lived in Canada virtually all our married life, he had absolutely no credit rating in the United States. We may as well have been criminals! Nobody trusted us financially except the owners of the house we were renting! For the longest time we were unable even to secure a telephone in the house, and once we did, it was months longer before we could call long-distance. Our budget was tight, so we kept the air conditioning to a minimum. Bob needed the minivan to go to work, so the kids and I rode our bikes a couple of miles to the local library so that they could use the internet. Ten houses down from ours in one direction was a beautiful grassy park and ten houses away in the other direction, a community swimming pool. It was really a wonderful setup.

*We were unwilling to move on with our lives just to find ourselves in a state of mere survival.*

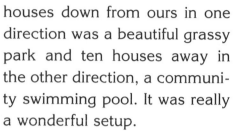

Outside of home, church became our addiction. We looked forward to every Sunday morning, Sunday evening, and Wednesday night service at Phoenix First Assembly. For one thing, we made some fast and firm friendships that God used tremendously in the months to come. More than that, though, being in a place of worship brought continued healing to us. Week after week, we would stand in God's presence holding each other's hands and weeping as we worshipped. Leo's Sunday school class was directly geared to marriages. We ate up every word, because even though life was getting a little less crazy, we still had an enormous amount of hurt to deal with.

Although we were still far from being completely healed, we knew the Healer and were beginning to recognize the times and the events, but mostly the relationships He would bring to aid us along this journey. Healing takes time. We were unwilling to move on with our lives and only merely survive. We wanted a thriving marriage and children who would be in awe at what God can do with two lives that are totally surrendered to Him. Patient trust was one of the lessons we had to learn time and again.

For me, the hurt expressed itself most often in a drive to be perfect. I still suffered from an innate need to make up for my stupid act. I didn't care how much it drained me; I was going to earn Bob's love back. I woke up early every morning, made sure I hugged and kissed Bob good-bye and told him I loved him. But I couldn't help the fact that I was wearing big pregnant clothes. I would stand at the door waving to him and watch as he drove off with a look of utter disgust on his face. Most of the time, I cried as soon as he left.

No matter what I did, I knew it wasn't enough. Several times a day I told him I loved him. I kept the house clean and welcoming. I made meals every night. I worked to keep the kids happy. But most of the times when I told Bob I loved him, he couldn't give the response I hoped for. Deep inside, I knew he loved me—his staying with me and his covering me proved that—but expressing his love in any tangible way seemed impossible for him at the time. I can't imagine how he felt inside, but for me, *it hurt like hell!*

Audrey kept telling me she loved me, but I couldn't get past what I saw with my eyes. Seeing her every day in maternity clothes with an increasingly rotund belly and knowing that I had not planted that seed stung me beyond words. Your imagination creates vivid imagery that will play itself repeatedly. The torment of thought with all of imagery is indescribable. How could she say, "I love you," when the evidence to the contrary was staring me in the face? How could she say she loved *me* when she had been with another person? You can't do something like that; it just doesn't make sense.

It's not that I didn't want her to say, "I love you"; I suppose I needed to hear it, even then. With me, it was more a gut reaction of disbelief: you love me? Yeah, right! If you loved me, you wouldn't have played around! If you loved me, you wouldn't have lied to me about where you were going and what you were doing! If you loved me, this wouldn't have happened! How can you say you love me after doing what you did? And now, all these desperate attempts to "prove" a love that I had always believed was beyond doubt!

Our love had always been open and abundant, so to go from that to this was a near hell on earth.

Audrey and I discovered that one of the immediate consequences of adultery was the rising up inside both of us of a strong feeling of being unlovable with each other. This is a side of adultery we rarely see in the movies or the TV dramas and sitcoms. Live fast, live loose, and live for pleasure, with no shame, no regrets, and no apologies! That's what our society tells us. The only problem is that we are not built that way emotionally. In reality, adultery takes a terrible toll in guilt, shame, anger, rejection, shattered self-esteem, and broken trust. In the midst of it all comes an overwhelming sense—for both parties—of being unlovable. Unfortunately, feeling unlovable often leads to desperation...and this quiet desperation to be loved is a dangerous thing.

Even calling these affairs "love" is hoping that this next relationship will satisfy the ache of a desperate heart that needs God instead of the counterfeit: fulfilling selfish lust through emotional highs and forbidden sex.

Adultery leaves both spouses feeling unlovable, which boils down to a deep sense of inadequacy. Whether the adulterous spouse or the offended spouse, both feel inadequate of holding the love of the other. That's how I felt, and I know Audrey did too.

*Adultery leaves both spouses feeling unlovable, which boils down to a deep sense of inadequacy.*

After I committed adultery, I felt unlovable because of what I had done. Until then I hadn't thought myself capable of something like that. I thought I was immune from such a "big" sin. After all, I was too smart, too wise, too involved, and too educated. Why would I want anything else? I didn't have to do anything this selfish. There was no good reason. I didn't feel unloved by my parents or by God or by Bob before all this happened.

In the aftermath of my adultery, I was so very angry at myself for screwing up my life, not to mention Bob's. I had messed up everything good that I had. What made it worse was Bob's rejection of me. Most of that first year, during the pregnancy, I felt very unloved by Bob, hugely rejected and punished, and who could blame him? Why should he love me when I was so unlovable? I couldn't even love myself.

My reaction was to go into "performance mode"; to do anything humanly possible to make up for the wrong I had done. That had always worked in the past, and it seemed the right thing to do. With my background, it was also the "automatic" thing to do. It was not necessarily a heart change. That would come later, over time.

Audrey's adultery had the effect on me of confirming what I had "known" in my heart since childhood—that I was unlovable. First of all, I was the second-born child in my family; I have an older brother. Since the firstborn was a boy, I was "supposed" to be a girl, at least in my mother's desire. That was one strike against me. Second, mine was an extremely difficult delivery. In those days, forceps were used routinely in childbirth, and when they pried me out, I had cuts over my eyes so that my eyes were swollen shut. My mother didn't even see my eyes until a couple of days after I was born. Third, I had a very large birthmark on my back. So, not only was I not the girl my mother wanted, I was an ugly boy!

When I was first placed in the nursery bassinet near my mother, she rolled over and wouldn't look at me. I was not what she wanted. These may have been her initial feelings, and this just confirms the truth that we have the greatest disappointments where we have placed unrealistic expectations. All through my life I have been shadowed by this sneaking suspicion that I am unlovable. Even though my mom loves me extravagantly, and our relationship is rich, an inner voice has always been there to tell me, "No matter how close and loving people are around you, it will all end eventually, and they will reject you and hurt you. If they ever discover what you are *really* like on the inside, they will not love you." As a result, in many ways I lived a very guarded life.

I was still very self-conscious about this even when Audrey and I were dating. My birthmark was an issue then. Audrey's adultery simply recalled everything I had thought about myself all these years: It would eventually come out someday. Our love was too good to be true.

*Men are wired by God to be the visionaries, the ones to give leadership and direction to their families.*

Over the four years of our growth and healing, as Audrey and I have shared our story at different conferences and meetings, I have become more and more convinced that this sense of worthlessness is a deeper and more widespread problem for men than most of us are willing to admit. Men are wired by God to be the visionaries, the ones to give leadership and direction to their families. Many men today, stuck in dead-end jobs or in careers they hate and confused or ignorant about what it really means to be a man, have lost their sense of vision, and with it, their sense of purpose. Without vision or purpose, and with no clear personal identity, these men feel lost and unworthy of esteem. Because they do not love themselves, they cannot believe that anyone else can truly love them.

During this time, we both had validated pain, but that pain was so different for each of us. It was important to grasp the wisdom God was imparting to us. We are not each other's answer, and we are not each other's enemy. Even though I tried not to see Audrey as my enemy, I couldn't embrace her. It hurt too much. In my quiet desperation, I wrestled with thoughts of anger and rage towards Audrey and a strong sense of failure. I felt destitute.

I'll never forget the drive to work one day. I really wanted to do it. I had been entertaining thoughts of suicide, never really saying the word but living with such pain and wondering when it would release its hold. The enemy of my soul was right there feeding me his lies that I was a complete failure and incapable of loving or being loved. Pain is a powerful motivator and can launch us into wholeness or drive us towards death. With the speed I was traveling on the freeways, I could so easily just turn the steering wheel into the embankment. I began seriously considering this as an option. While I was stopped at a red light, a familiar song came on the radio, one I had not heard for years.

*When you're up against a struggle that shatters all your dreams,*

*and your hopes have been cruelly crushed by Satan's manifested scheme,*

*And you feel the urge within you to submit to earthly fears,*

*Don't let the faith you're standing in seem to disappear.*

*Praise the Lord!*

*He can work with those who praise Him.*

*Praise the Lord!*

*For our God inhabits praise.*

*Praise the Lord!*

*For the chains that seem to bind you*

*Serve only to remind you*

*That they drop powerless behind you*

*When you praise Him.*[i]

That morning I was so loved by my Lord as He came to me at my point of near despair and silenced my tormentors with His presence. I entered the freeway with tears rolling down my face, realizing I had just been rescued.

Engaging myself in praise and worship became essential to my healing process. The words of my mouth and the meditations of my heart needed continual monitoring. I realized I was less spiritual than I thought I was. Too often we talk about prayer, personal devotion, and quiet times alone with Him when in actuality they are something we rarely involve ourselves in. So with great purpose and determination I pursued the Lord with my whole being. I prayed and sang aloud continuously, placing my good intentions and thoughts into actions.

Fear of being inadequate and unlovable feeds the quiet desperation so many men live under day after day. Deep inside they suspect that something is wrong with them, but they have no idea what it is or what to do about it. So, instead of discovering its source, they try to ignore it or camouflage it in some way, hoping not to be discovered.

Inevitably, this sense of inadequacy comes out in a variety of ways. Some men withdraw from their wives, becoming insensitive and unresponsive, leaving their wives starved for love and wondering where *they* have failed. Other men become domineering and even abusive, taking their inadequacy out on those closest to them. There are others who become so passive and docile that they virtually relinquish their responsibilities as a husband and father.

*Fear of being inadequate and unlovable feeds the quiet desperation so many men live under day after day.*

The years of healing since Audrey's adultery have been a *huge* unveiling for me. When all of this started, I thought it was all about Audrey. Then, suddenly, it became all about me. Leo recognized this right away. That is why he focused so much on *my* attitudes and actions. It seemed as though in every counseling session he singled me out and for the longest time I thought he was being so unfair.

One of my biggest struggles, particularly in the earliest days after the affair, was with my "need" to know details. I constantly badgered Audrey with questions of why, *why*, WHY! I wanted to know, I needed to know, I *had* to know…no…as the wronged husband I had the *right* to know every stinking, sordid detail: When? Where? How many times? These questions and related imaginings tormented my mind. In my anger and injured self-righteousness, I could not see (and at that time probably would not have cared) that every harsh question and bitter accusation that I flung at Audrey diminished her a little more.

I needed to change patterns in my thinking and behavior. My insistence on knowing details and my questions of her intent were prolonging the healing process in our relationship. In fact, when I kept asking her why she had done this, I was placing myself in the seat of judgment. Whenever we ask the question "why," we are judging another's heart.

Until I could let go of it, forgiveness could not complete its work. Every time I demanded more details from Audrey, I was really saying, "I haven't forgiven you." This was never my intention. I didn't recognize that I was being unforgiving. I just didn't want it to happen again, and I was unconvinced that she knew the seriousness of what she had done. If Audrey had known the seriousness of what she had done, she never would have done it in the first place.

Knowing *why* Audrey committed adultery would not change the fact that it happened. Regardless of how natural a desire it may seem, the desire to know "why" ultimately is a fruitless pursuit. Asking "why?" locks us in the past, which causes us to miss what God is saying and doing in the present, and keeps us from being prepared for the future.

Asking "what now?" puts us in a mind-set to hear from God. It enables us to respond to the prompting of the Holy Spirit *right now* to do what we are supposed to be doing *right now*. The "why?" question hangs us up every time. All it leads to is frustration. When we learn to resist the "why?" and instead ask "what now?" we bring glory to God because we are surrendering our presumptuous "need to know" for simple trust in the grace of God.

Forgiveness is not forgetting. It would be humanly impossible to forget what happened. Forgiveness is not a price I pay because I owe it. It's also not an analgesic that stops the pain. Forgiveness becomes a gift that I give myself.

While Bob was struggling between "why?" and "what now?" I was in the middle of a struggle of my own making. Sin took me further than I ever wanted to go and kept me there longer than I wanted to stay. I'm convinced that the enemy sought to destroy our marriage and our family. But even more than that, he wanted to go even a step further and bring separation between myself and God. Ultimately, he hated the love relationship I had with Jesus. The enemy didn't want our marriage to work, but even more, he didn't want me or Bob to experience God's love. His plan to make us feel naked, ashamed, and disqualified would lead us down the dark path of endless guilt and leave us defeated, hopeless, and useless.

Thankfully, this plan didn't work. Through the darkest hours of this journey, I knew God still loved me. I knew I wasn't alone. I didn't necessarily "feel" close to God, but I didn't doubt His love. I truly believe the enemy hates it when we understand unconditional love. There is nothing more powerful or redeeming.

Everything that God had planted to bear fruit in my life was an insult to the enemy. Every potential of growth and effectiveness was a threat to the enemy's schemes. Through this entire season of my journey, I have never had the temptation to stop loving God, or believing the lie that He didn't love me. But I say that with fear and trembling, because I know that if the adulterous relationship would have continued, I don't know what the ramifications would have been. I know that there is always hope of restoration and redemption, but I also know that the journey would have been even more painful than it already was.

*The enemy hates it when we understand unconditional love. There is nothing more powerful or redeeming.*

Journaling had been so important to me for so many years, even being part of my regular prayer pattern. It just seemed that I could express my truest and deepest feelings so well through the written word. More important, it was through journaling that the voice of the Lord came most clearly to me. Unfortunately, I had not made a single journal entry since that sad day when I found Bob reading my journals and angrily threw them away.

Now, without my journal, I sometimes felt like I had lost connection with Jesus. At the most critical time in my life, when I knew I needed God in my life more than ever, I denied my most important instrument for personal expression and for hearing God's voice. I began to crave the opportunity to journal again and to use that venue to pour out my feelings. In the recent past, my journals had betrayed me, or so I thought. I prayed for God to forgive me for my ill feelings on that day and asked Him if I was ready to journal again. I knew He would answer. He always does. Faithfulness is God's very character.

The next day, after coming home from a bike ride, I saw a bag hanging on our outside doorknob. Upon opening it, I found an absolutely beautiful empty journal with a picture on the cover of Jesus the Great Shepherd. Inside was a card from one of my new friends at church, Shawna. Her note was filled with words of love and support that could have come only straight from the Holy Spirit. Tears began to stream down my face. The journal was from a new acquaintance who grew into one of my dearest friends, but the message from Jesus Himself was loud and clear: "Audrey, it's time to start journaling again."

My spiritual journey continued, and although I was walking through the valley of the shadow of death, I had no need to fear evil, for my Shepherd was with me. His rod and His staff would comfort me.

One day, after hanging laundry on the clothesline (our dryer didn't work!), I sat down, opened my new journal and began to write. Oh, the joy to let my pen fly and my thoughts and feelings and questions pour onto the pages in a gushing tide! One question caused me to pause and reflect: "Why am I not sick with this pregnancy?" I was well through the first trimester, yet had not experienced a trace of weariness or any of the nausea that had all but laid me out during my three prior pregnancies! What was going on?

As I pondered this wonder, God spoke into my heart an answer that is forever etched in the depths of my soul: "Audrey, with all that we are going through together in this season of your life, there is no way that you would have the capacity to carry a baby. I have been carrying this baby for you."

Suddenly, that explained everything: the ease of this pregnancy, my lack of sickness, and my ability to move heavy furniture, fight through emotional trauma, and work from morning to night without getting tired. I thought I had known God's grace before; I got to know it a lot more deeply that day! "Amazing grace, how sweet the sound that saved a wretch like me...." I was on my way back to letting God whisper tenderly in my ear. I was on my way home!

My struggle was far from over, however. As my belly grew, my fear and shame continued to grow as well. It pained Bob to see my pregnant body; I could see it in his face. No matter how hard I tried to be perfect and earn his love, I still felt punished and ashamed. On the way home from counseling one morning, I just wanted the pain to end. I wanted to go on with life, and I asked Bob what it would take. "Do you want me to tell the world that I'm an adulterous woman?" I opened the car window and desperately screamed, "I committed adultery!" It was a sad moment full of extreme anxiety and hopelessness. Silently and tearfully, I begged God to heal our marriage. This was not the quick fix I had hoped for.

It was during those times when I felt most unloved and rejected that I was most vulnerable to temptation. I knew that if I were to call that phone number or email that address I would hear that familiar voice and get the affirmation I craved. After all the hell that this relationship had brought into my life and marriage, there were moments when it *still* had a grip on me emotionally. Deception dies hard. I struggled with this for five or six months. When times got the hardest, Molly, Leo's wife, prayed for me. My friend Shawna gave me perspective and encouragement that one day I would be disgusted by the whole thing and not be tempted at all. I wanted to believe her. I hung on to that hope, because that is exactly what I wanted.

*No matter how hard I tried to be perfect and earn his love, I still felt punished and ashamed.*

Another thing that helped me keep going was this baby inside of me. I kept remembering that many mighty men in the Bible were conceived in unusual or even sinful circumstances, because God loves to show His redeeming power. The Bible says that even David was conceived in sin. What that means precisely, we don't know, but it could mean that he was an illegitimate child. This would help explain why he was left in the field watching the sheep while all his brothers were brought before Samuel, who was looking for the next king of Israel to anoint.

So many of the world-changing, earth-shaking kind of guys had to live through tough circumstances, and I hung on to that. God is a Redeemer. He loves to turn our mistakes into something good. It certainly wasn't God's will for the adultery to take place, and yet I knew He already had a purpose for the baby I was carrying. I remember praying, "Lord, there's a baby in here whom You are going to use. I know You are going to redeem this."

I didn't have a dream for our marriage at that point. I wanted it to be okay, but I had only the faintest hope that it could ever be great again. I begged God to make that happen, but I confess that I didn't have a lot of faith to believe for it. Because I had failed so miserably, I didn't deserve a great marriage.

The first nine months after our "terrorist attack" was God's rescue mission. Like a bullet shot right to the heart, death was approaching quickly and suddenly. God's surgery was like taking a sharp knife and with precision and understanding removing the obstruction; in this case, a hardness of heart that manifested itself through sexual sin. First, all that is seen is the wound, which was caused by the sexual sin, but it was our hard hearts that made room for this, and changing our hearts became crucial to the healing process. Serious wounds, once healed, often leave a scar. Our lives would be forever scarred by what I had done, but a scar is evidence of healing. Just as a broken bone that has mended is stronger at the broken places, so scar tissue is tougher than regular skin and also protects the site of the wound better. Although Bob and I were in no position to see it at the time, this war wound in our own marriage would become a testimony of hope to others that they can survive adultery or other major relationship-killers and, even more, thrive and experience the full benefits of walking in covenant. We have learned so much when it comes to sexual issues.

This physical union is far beyond one-dimensional; it encompasses my whole being. The world around us promotes casual sex as the most adventurous when, in reality, it's the most destructive. In actuality, when love between a couple deepens and grows, so does the sexual union. As Bob and I grow together as friends, and as we have committed to join in prayer each day, face to face, looking into each other's eyes, our intimacy is maximized. We approach ever closer to what God initially created this masterful union to entail.

*The world around us promotes casual sex as the most adventurous when, in reality, it's the most destructive.*

Because we are three-dimensional, when one partner isn't involved in the relationship with his or her mind, but rather fantasizes about another person, that dimension is subtracted, making the intimacy "less than." As we allow God to help us control and renew the way we think, we will begin to involve ourselves on a much higher level.

Sex cannot be selfish. It's contrary to why it was created. God created sex to be enjoyed within the covenant of marriage between one man and one woman, a relationship that gives fully and loves unconditionally. A relationship is the mutual sharing of life one with another. Selfishness is never satisfied in its cravings, but always demands more and more. One-dimensional physical sex leaves one feeling empty, and it keeps one looking for more. This is the enemy's way of destroying God's plan for marriage in covenant.

One of the benefits of Bob's job was medical insurance, which is always a good thing—especially when a baby is on the way! I went for my first doctor's appointment when the baby was about nineteen weeks along. In the waiting room, a girl seated next to me asked me whether I suspected it was a boy or a girl. I told her that I didn't really know, but that I wanted a girl in the biggest way. She commented that she was sure it was a girl; not to worry.

A girl *would* be so much easier; a girl like me. Less than ten minutes later, I found out that God doesn't always allow us to take the easiest route possible! When the doctor told me the baby was a boy, I asked him if I could change it. He chuckled and said, "You're not in Sweden, honey!"

All fun aside, I was completely overwhelmed! I couldn't handle a boy! How could God let this happen? I was angry and confused. And I had exactly one hour to get my attitude right before I picked up Janelle from a church function. Her saving grace in this whole thing was the thought that she was going to get a little sister. She and I were always drawn to those pretty little girl clothes, and having a baby so late in life, I knew I would have lots of time alone with this new little one. A baby girl could be my best little girlfriend!

Suddenly, I saw my attitude from God's perspective. What horrible pride to think that I had a better idea than God Himself! To think that I had a plan that exceeded His highest, just to fit my selfish desires! I repented quickly, but still felt sad. I asked God to give me a creative way to tell Janelle that it was a boy, or else give me the opportunity to keep it a secret for awhile. As always, God came through!

When I picked Janelle up from the church function, she jumped in the car and the first words out of her mouth were, "Did you find out whether it was a boy or a girl?" I exclaimed in shrill excitement, "Yes, I did! Janelle, you're going to be my *only* little girl forever!" Janelle was ecstatic that day, and has been ever since.

On the day I needed it most, Shawna had given me a fresh, empty journal. I came home this day to find another bag on our door handle, filled this time with the cutest little boy clothes, all wrapped up with love and understanding. It was his very first set of clothes! They were for a boy, and we were going to be okay with that. Really okay.

A *boy?* Audrey's having a *boy?* That really blew my plans out of the water! I really thought God was in my corner on this one. We had a home and a church; I had a job and was doing a little better. Just when I was starting to think I could make it...a *boy?* I was as startled as Audrey. I had really hoped for a girl. And now to find out it was a boy! What if the baby looked like this other person? The child could be a constant and painful reminder of everything that had happened. I had it all figured out; with a girl, Audrey could do all sorts of little girl things with her, and I could keep my distance and not be as attached. I'm so glad I could deal with these disappointments months before meeting our baby. My own mother was disappointed that I was a boy, and now I had an opportunity to resist letting history repeat itself. This was my opportunity for growth, for me to again trust God that He was giving me the greatest gift I could ever have.

I remember coming home from work one day and seeing Audrey in the kitchen, GREAT with child, and Janelle rubbing her tummy and talking to the baby. Janelle must have sensed a cold chill from across the room because she looked at me, and I could see her stuck between two worlds: one where she sees her Dad's pain and the other where she loves her Mom and adores the expected baby. Not wanting her to choose between her mother's feelings and me, I said quickly, "Honey, you just love that baby with everything you've got."

*There was nothing in my experience that Jesus did not experience as well. Pain, hurt, anger, betrayal—He knew them all.*

This was so different from our other pregnancies, because I wasn't part of this one! I felt robbed; violated! A thief stole in and took something that wasn't his to take, something that Audrey and I could never get back again. For months I believed that all our dreams were gone! I even felt like our first seventeen years of marriage were a fallacy. I couldn't remember all the countless, happy memories we had as a family. How truly blinding pain is, and the enemy takes his opportunity to feed lie after lie. When you're in pain, that's all you can think about. Any romantic vision we ever had of our marriage was gone, tainted, probably forever. We were "damaged goods"

now. The beautiful bride I married...how could I ever fully love her again the way I once did? I already had three wonderful children. God, would it be possible for me to love this new baby the way I knew I should? I was scared. I didn't want to fail.

I used to think that my situation was the one and only; that no one else had ever gone where I had gone or felt what I had felt. That was a lie from the mouth of the enemy! I learned that the Lord knew exactly where I was and how I felt. There was nothing in my experience that Jesus did not experience as well. Pain, hurt, anger, betrayal—He knew them all.

Desperate people should not be alone. We need others through times like these and reaching out to church and community brings safety and comfort. We could never adequately thank the people God used to rescue us. When we were reaching out for a lifeline, there were willing people available to love us and accept us, even in our state of brokenness.

Shawna and my other friend, Cindy, threw a huge baby shower for me. I was overwhelmed with love in a way that assured me that everything was going to be okay. There were so many loving people there, smiling, celebrating, and generously giving gifts to this new baby. These two girls were the only friends I had who fully knew what was going on, and it was as though God sent them on a mission to love me unconditionally and act as though we had all been best friends since childhood. I went home from the shower that day with absolutely every single thing I needed to take care of the baby. This was a wonderful blessing, considering the tight budget we were living on at the time. Once again, I marveled at the ways God shows His love for us.

According to Arizona law, the baby, when born, would be Bob's legal son because he was the husband of the home. As the day approached, there was still so much fear of the unknown. Would everyone figure it out once he was born? Would people accept us once they knew what had transpired? Would Bob be able to love him? Would I be able to bond with him? With each passing day our fears grew. We rarely talked about it, but our silence confirmed that we were both worried.

With one month still to go before the projected due date, the unexpected happened. God's endless mercy came through again, as He saw our deep fears grow with each passing day. It was a Saturday night around midnight. We had just returned from a huge dinner at Leo and Molly's. Much to our surprise, my water broke. My fear turned to uncontrollable shaking as we drove to the hospital. I wasn't scared of the pain of childbirth; I knew what that was like and knew I could handle it. I was scared for my own destiny.

Bob and I had invited my mom to be in the room when this little one was born. Of course, when I went into labor early, she was still in Canada. I called her about 1:30 in the morning and asked her to start praying. She did more than just pray; she packed her bags, got on a plane, and was in Phoenix and by my side within ten hours, by 11:30 that morning! I was in labor until 6:30 that evening.

⊹⊨⊨⊹

Here we were in the hospital. Audrey was in labor and soon to give birth. Janelle really wanted to come, and I'm glad she was there. I'm glad my dad was there, too. He was great through the whole thing; my silent strength.

As for me, I was watching Audrey going through her labor pains and—I'm sorry, but I just couldn't help myself—I was thinking, *Oh, I hope that hurt! I hope you feel every contraction!* Then they gave Audrey an epidural, and she *really* mellowed out! In fact, she basically slept through most of the rest. My dad, in his inimitable way, said, "This was exciting before, but now it's like watching paint dry! It looks like the show's over. Let's get some lunch!" My dad continually came through for me, and his love for both of us was strongly evident and brought strength to one of the scariest days of my life.

Audrey and I had agreed that I would name the baby. Janelle and I had found a baby name book. I already knew what his first name would be. I chose his middle name the same day he was born. All that was left now was for this little boy to make his appearance.

We didn't have to wait long. At 6:30 pm on Sunday, October 7, 2001, our son was born. That's right—*our* son. At six pounds, seven ounces, he was perfect, beautiful. This divine gift from God, His trophy of grace, made his entrance into this world: Robert Theodore Meisner. Theodore means "gift of God," and that is just what he is. I chose to give him *my* name, Robert, because I didn't want him ever to doubt a day of his life whose son he is. He is *my* boy, and I love him with all my heart! He is a *chosen* son—doubly chosen—chosen by God for us, and chosen by *me* as *my* son. A new Meisner had arrived.

Audrey bonded with Robert instantly. The day after he was born, we were together in the room, gazing at our new little boy. Janelle said, "It's amazing how something so beautiful can come from something so absolutely awful." Audrey agreed. God's grace and mercy are truly awesome! There was no question that this was the beginning of a beautiful new relationship. He was the one chosen to join our family. He had lots of dark hair, a sweet little face, and a countenance of perfect peace. Our gift.

### Endnote

1. © 1977 Bug and Bear Music (ASCAP) and Home Sweet Home Music (BMI). International copyright secured. All rights reserved. Used by permission.

# Chapter Five

# Healed

As little Robert—*our* son—grew, our relationship seemed to turn a corner for the better. His presence helped bring Audrey and me closer together in a way that only a newborn baby can. There were still questions and uncertainties as we faced the future, but one thing we knew for sure: we wanted our marriage to be even *better* than it was before. We had no idea what it would be like, but we were willing to take the journey to discover.

I wanted to hate the sin so badly. Repentance and seeing my sin for what it really is go hand in hand. I'm very thankful that today I do hate the sin. I never think about this individual or wonder what he's doing or what he's thinking. I don't fixate on any memories of the past of our time together. And I certainly don't ever see shadows of him in our precious little boy. This is nothing short of a miracle. My prayer has been answered.

If God had unveiled the total ugliness of sin all at once, it would have crushed me. Instead, I have chosen to fall on Him and allow myself to be broken. *"The sacrifice you want is a broken spirit. A broken and repentant heart, O God, you will not despise"* (Psalm 51:17, NLT). In truth, this is the power of brokenness: the power to repent as often as necessary without shame and without hiding some of the truth. I had nothing to lose because my Lord knew it all even before I spoke. Love covers a multitude of sins, and He has affirmed me in His overwhelming love, acceptance, and utter forgiveness. With His heart of love, He reveals areas where sin has brought lost intimacy between

*In truth, this is the power of brokenness: the power to repent as often as necessary without shame and without hiding some of the truth.*

us. In my own heart, these areas are usually rooted in pride. As I confess my need for His indwelling presence in my life, He gives me grace. *"God opposes the proud but gives grace to the humble"* (James 4:6, NIV). May I never forget my need for Him.

We had been in Phoenix less than two years when I found out that my job was being transferred to Pittsburgh, Pennsylvania. Ron invited and encouraged me to move with it and become a vital part of a Christian broadcasting station there.

The only problem was that we thoroughly enjoyed our life in Phoenix. Our church life was thriving, and we had made many new and dear friends. Our kids were happy in school, and we *loved* the hot weather. Audrey told me that one day on her way to a U.S. Immigration appointment, as she walked down the palm-tree-lined street, she thanked God from the bottom of her heart for letting her, a "snow-infested" girl, live in such a place. As for me, I once said, "It would take an angel from heaven appearing to me in person to ever get me to move out of Phoenix."

In the end, the opportunity to influence a nation through broadcasting pulled us too strongly. I loved working for Ron Hembree, and the fit seemed right. Finally we decided that if we loved it so much in Phoenix, and God had taken such good care of us, He would do the same in Pittsburgh. I moved early, and Audrey and the kids spent the summer at her parents' home in Winnipeg.

We missed each other desperately and found ourselves constantly questioning our decision. Our house in Phoenix wasn't selling, and I was living in the basement of a small home in the outskirts of Pittsburgh. Soon, it was August—time to get the kids enrolled in school for the fall term, so we made our final move to Pittsburgh. Even though we weren't able to buy a home yet, the six of us could all live in the basement together.

Audrey tried so hard to love it. She tried so hard to be okay in that basement with the four kids. As a prairie girl, the hills and winding roads of western Pennsylvania were very unfamiliar to her, and she found herself feeling very closed in.

It wasn't just her or the surroundings; it was the same for all of the children as well. It was like a foot trying to fit into a glove. We squeezed and squeezed; we smiled and met many precious and beautiful people, but it wasn't working easily. School was starting the following week, and we didn't even know where the kids would be attending. Audrey's parents flew in for the weekend to be guests on the show. That's when the crazy chain of events started happening.

We woke up one morning to find that Chris, our oldest son, was missing. He had been sleeping on the couch in a sleeping bag, and it was empty. It was very early in the morning, with the sun barely out, and the rest of the family was all sleeping. Where was Chris? We woke Janelle up, and she told us that Chris had talked about going for a walk the night before. Now we began to get scared. Chris didn't know the area, and it would have been pitch dark all night. Who knows what could have happened? We phoned the hospitals and the police, and then prayed and hoped for the best.

About an hour later, the police squad car was in our driveway. We were watching out the front window when all of a sudden Chris came walking casually up the driveway. Talk about relief! Chris had no idea what we were going through. As it turned out, he had left for his walk only a short time before we discovered that he was gone. He had been gone for an hour and a half and had expected to be back before anyone else woke up. He had spent the time praying about his future. His heart was confused, and he was seeking answers from his heavenly Father.

The day before Audrey's mom and dad were to go back to Winnipeg, Chris took them aside and asked if he could move back to Winnipeg with them. He simply couldn't handle this last move emotionally, and knowing that his lifelong friends were in Winnipeg in a familiar high school was too much to resist. Sure, this wasn't the first time a sixteen-year-old moved away from his family, but it caused us to recognize how much he was hurting and how much he wanted a secure place to call home. We didn't have the heart to separate as a family. There was so much we had been through, and the kids had given up so much without one word of complaint. After much turmoil, I decided that although I was in the middle of a dream job situation with exceptional colleagues, my family came first. I resigned my job, and the family moved back to Winnipeg within a matter of days.

*The most profound reality I can embrace is that I can trust Him. Completely.*

The thing I missed most in our relationship was laughter. I'd always loved the freedom of uncontained laughter and spontaneous adventure. Even though we were enjoying each other more and more, I could still feel sadness deep within and was cautious in our journey together. God loves complete restoration even more than I do, but I had to trust Him and be patient. This was easier said than done! This wasn't going to happen my way, and it wasn't going to take place on my timetable. It was vital that I give up control in every area of my life. *The most profound reality I can embrace is that I can trust Him. Completely. God is not mad at me, and His ways are always higher than mine.*

133

Shortly after we had moved to Phoenix, I had phoned Lois Burkett and told her we were now living in the city. I then proceeded to tell her that I needed her to be my second mom because I was in a lot of trouble. I first got to know Lois when I was a young girl and she was a guest on my parents' program. We had stayed in contact through the years, and I knew that she loved me unconditionally.

This was another of God's divine appointments. Lois had immediately taken Bob and me under her wing. She is a pastor to pastors and an experienced counselor with a wonderful ministry of helping people in trouble. She loved us as her own. As it turned out, even in a city as large as Phoenix, she lived only blocks away from our newfound home! God sends many timely gifts to us in a lifetime, and His gift of Lois' love is one we will never forget.

One thing the Lord revealed to me during those months of counseling with Lois was that I needed to grow up in many ways. Being the youngest in my family and having a carefree personality, I thought I could have the attitude of a young girl forever. Growing up meant owning up to my mistakes. It also meant accepting the consequences of my actions. My conscience had to come fully alive. I needed to learn how to discern clearly between right and wrong and to choose the right. That was hard enough, but the next part was harder: I had to learn how to suffer.

Whenever we seek to obey God and do what we know is right, a part of us will always suffer: our flesh. The Bible calls it dying to self. We don't have to physically get on a cross as Jesus did, but we do have to take up our cross spiritually and die to the desires of a sinful nature: what *we* want, what *we* think, and how *we* feel. The lie is that if I obey I'll miss out on something, and there will be lack…lack of fun, lack of enjoyment, and lack of spontaneous adventure. The truth is that Jesus came that I might have life, and have it in abundance. This is where my *real* life in God begins to thrive. My *true* life is hidden in Christ Jesus.

> *Surrender is the pathway to victory, yet we resist surrender because in our minds it means defeat.*

Searching my heart meant learning to understand the true motives behind my actions. Taking responsibility for my sin meant examining my heart deeply. King David was a man after God's own heart, yet he committed adultery with Bathsheba. Psalm 51 is the prayer of repentance that David wrote after he was confronted with the reality of his sin. Rather than hide it or deny it, David acknowledged his sin and asked God for cleansing: *"Create in me a clean heart, O God, and renew a steadfast spirit within me. Do not cast me away from Your presence, and do not take Your Holy Spirit from me. Restore to me the joy of Your salvation, and uphold me by Your generous Spirit. Then I will teach transgressors Your ways, and sinners shall be converted to You"* (Psalm 51:10-13).

Surrender is the pathway to victory, yet we resist surrender because in our minds it means defeat. But the only way to achieve spiritual victory is by surrendering to God our wills, our desires, our thoughts, our plans, and our insistence on having our own way. We surrender because we can trust Him. We know that He has our best interest in mind.

How do you rekindle lost love? How do you save a marriage devastated by infidelity and betrayal? How do you protect a marriage from the determined attack of an implacable enemy? How can a marriage not only survive but *thrive* in a culture of quiet desperation that hasn't a clue to the nature of true love? The key is to tap into true love at its supernatural source—God. This requires humility, honesty, surrender, and obedience on a daily basis, allowing God to take you on your own personal journey to wholeness.

God designed us to depend on Him daily, and when we don't, our lives are out of kilter. The more we *depend* on God the better we come to *know* Him, and the better we know Him, the *closer* we draw to Him. The closer we draw to Him, the more we *love* Him. Dependence, knowledge, closeness, love...these are all *relational* words that help to define intimacy.

Satan counterfeits with *false intimacy*. How does it compare? Instead of dependence there is *co-dependency*; instead of knowledge, *deception*; instead of closeness, *superficial affection*; and instead of love, *lust*.

Throughout my life, I have always wanted God in a big way. I used to read the Gospels and think about the disciples who walked with Him, spoke with Him, and lived with Him day in and day out. I wanted the same thing. Even more, I wanted to be His "special" one, like the "disciple whom Jesus loved." Long ago I decided I wanted *that* spot. I never told a soul, and to be frank, I felt kind of bad about it, as if I was selfish for even desiring such a thing.

Then I heard a message that changed everything. Our pastor in Phoenix, Tommy Barnett, preached a sermon one day about being God's favorite. He described John and his relationship with Jesus, and then said that we can *all* have that place and position. In fact, the only book in the Bible that talks about John that way is in the Gospel of John! This was John's *own* perspective of his relationship with Jesus; a perspective that is available to every one of us. I was free to be His favorite!

God uses marriage as a picture of our relationship with Him. If I desire true intimacy with God, it is only natural to desire true intimacy with Bob in our marriage. It's okay to want it all when it comes to marriage as long as I am willing to give it all! True intimacy in marriage suffers when a husband and wife become blind to the beautiful qualities of character, strength, and inner grace that once drew them together. How do they restore intimacy? By finding ways to make themselves irresistible to each other again! *The most irresistible quality is a heart surrendered to God.*

Because God seeks deep and thorough healing for His children, He sometimes brings us through new layers of healing at unexpected times and in unanticipated ways. This happened to me and Bob shortly after our family moved back to Winnipeg.

It was Valentine's Day, 2003: two years since that pathetic day when I tried to let Bob know I loved him through presents and balloons after confessing my sin of adultery. Robert was now sixteen months old. Two of our very close friends, Pam Thum and Stephen Marshall, were in town as guests on *It's A New Day*, as well two new guests we hadn't met before: Dr. Don and Mary Colbert. Pam and Steve were one of the first couples we told about the adultery and pregnancy, and their intense love and faithful prayers carried us through many long nights and painful days. It was Friday night after a big week, and Mom had cooked an extravagant dinner for all of us in her home.

That Valentine's Day is marked in my heart forever. After dinner, Dr. Don began ministering to all of us. As he was praying for me, he identified acute grief that was locked up deep in my heart. He went on to explain that we all go through grief, but that this was something different. It was the result of extreme loss of something or someone, and this grief was locked inside. I looked around the room, and everyone was quiet. I then proceeded to tell the story of what had happened just two short years before. My grief was locked in because I hadn't yet forgiven myself for what took place. I was holding in the sorrow and pain and keeping it close to my heart. On the outside, few people would notice. God knew, however, and I quickly discovered that I was in the middle of yet another divine appointment.

Dr. Don told me that the key to unlocking my grief would be found in changing my belief system. He instructed me to repeat after him: "It is good for me to get rid of this grief. It is good for Bob that I get rid of this grief. God's plan is that I get rid of this grief. I need to get rid of this grief. I want to get rid of this grief." So far, all was going well. I repeated his statements easily—until he got to the last one: "I deserve to get rid of this grief." I couldn't say it. Deep down I still believed I needed to be punished. I didn't deserve to be completely free. *But God had a different idea.* He loved me so much that He had orchestrated this night in this place with these people so that I could be liberated.

We prayed to correct my belief system, and I finally understood from God's perspective that I deserved to get rid of my grief. I finally accepted my place as His daughter who had always been forgiven. I no longer had to hold on to this grief. The next step was to begin to feel my suppressed grief...deeply.

The reason for this is that we try to manage, suppress, subdue, and starve painful thoughts by filling our minds with other things. Meanwhile the memory festers deep inside and can resurface at any moment. Someone says something or something happens and this festering wound rises up at exactly the wrong time, resulting in outbursts of rage and anger. We can control such memories for only so long. We all like to control our emotions and express only the ones that are socially acceptable. Phrases like, "I love you," "I don't like that," and "That tastes good," are all fine and good, but deep inside are conflicting feelings. On this night I was asked to feel every one of them. I needed to go as deep as I could.

This process was not to bring up or glorify ugly emotions, but to bring the hidden pain to the surface. God wants to go to the deep crevices of our hearts and love us in those places. It is our deepest wounds and hurts that He wants to heal by ministering His unconditional love to us. Allowing Jesus to go to our deep or hidden memories brings the healing salve of the Lord to the festering wound. Paul wrote in Ephesians 3:18: *"And may you have the power to understand, as all God's people should, how wide, how long, how high, and how deep his love really is"* (NLT). He wants to go deep with His love, and we don't think we deserve this. We think, "I blew it. I messed up. I need to earn it." That's a wrong belief system, and it prevents us from letting God remove the "hooks" in our life that trigger anger, bitterness, and self-pity.

*Allowing Jesus to go to our deep or hidden memories brings the healing salve of the Lord to the festering wound.*

Dr. Don asked me to remember the hard things, like how it felt to tell Bob and to tell the kids and how it felt to know that I had completely betrayed them and had no way to turn back the clock. As I thought on these things, I began to feel the reality of what I had done as never before. My feelings of regret turned into wailing. For the first time, I saw the full devastation of my sin and grieved over it. I saw my sin the way God did, and then let it go. As I grieved and allowed Jesus to love me in each painful thought or memory, I released it out of my system. To say this was intense would be an understatement! The whole process lasted probably an hour. Afterwards, there was such a sweet presence of the Lord in the room! I wasn't disqualified. God turned my mourning into dancing! He gave me beauty for ashes.

The night after Audrey was so powerfully released from her grief, I experienced a deliverance of my own. As with Audrey's repentance, I had gone through my forgiveness in layers. Incident after incident, thought after thought, I would choose to forgive, hoping that one day the pain and torment would stop.

Once again, the Colberts were God's instruments for bringing healing. As in Audrey's case, the first thing they did was challenge my belief system. I needed to be reassured of my identity in Christ: who I am in Him and who He is in me.

Next, we dealt with the forgiveness issue. I knew I had to forgive. I wanted to forgive. It was good for me, it was good for Audrey, and it was good for everybody else. As the Colberts began to pray, they asked me to remember everything and feel it as deeply as possible: every emotion and every thought, even the worst and most unimaginable.

I talk with a lot of other men who have been through the agony of their wives committing adultery. Most of them have never seen their wives in bed with another man. I had formed a picture in my mind, almost like a video, of Audrey with the other guy. Every act she was involved in, I created it in my own mind down to the last detail: where they were, what took place, what they said, how they touched, etc. The Bible calls this "vain imagination." Second Corinthians 10:5 tells us to take *"every thought into captivity to the obedience of Christ."* We get so caught up in vain imaginations. Sure, these things are true; they did take place, but these thoughts, these "vain imaginations" create a reality that affects our bodies. Our physical bodies respond to these imaginary visuals just as if we were seeing them for real right before our eyes.

Dr. Don began praying, and I began revisiting that imagination. Soon I was weeping and crying and letting go, and it was all being lifted from me. Jesus had always been there, right in the middle of my pain. I realized that there was nothing left. Surprisingly, I couldn't feel the hurtful memories anymore. I couldn't cry anymore. I thought that was it. Dr.

Don clearly knew there was more. He said, "There has got to be something you aren't dealing with."

Then the Holy Spirit brought it to my memory. I had created a visual of the time Audrey had gotten pregnant; their last time together. I had every detail formed in my mind. I already knew where and when, and I visualized the rest in my head. I believed my life would have been okay if that one event had never happened. I had to revisit it. When I forgave that act of adultery it was as if a dam broke. These trapped, deadly emotions were released, and His river of life and love swept over me. All of a sudden it wasn't just about me. For all this time, my self-righteous attitude had blinded me from seeing the other side. I saw Audrey's hurt and loss for the first time. Compassion for Audrey overwhelmed me, and I saw with new eyes how my beautiful bride was violated in such an ugly circumstance.

It was powerful. The poisonous venom of bitterness dropped out of me, and i became whole. We fell into each other's arms and wept. This embrace was like none other. In that significant moment, we recaptured untainted and true love. It was freedom as we had never felt before. After going through this process of radical forgiveness, Audrey instantly felt safe again for the first time in years. There was no more need to perform. Our relationship was at rest.

My unforgiveness and Audrey's grief and inability to forgive herself had restricted us from being the "whole" people God intended us to be. If we weren't whole, we wouldn't be able to have that "10" marriage that we longed for. Before these deep-seated issues were released in our lives, we were doing okay. We would not have known that we needed prayer for them. The Lord knew, however, and He made us aware so that we were able to repent for holding onto them for so long, and we received cleansing and forgiveness.

None of this was natural; all of it was supernatural. Love Audrey as Christ loves the church? I couldn't do it. Not alone. When I connected to the source—Christ—I could begin to love her that way because I saw with new eyes. It really is the life of Christ living through me.

These deadly emotions affected my physical body

*God doesn't just want our soul and spirit to be healed, but our physical body as well.*

as well! Not loving ourselves and wanting to die cause our system to shut down. Our bodies naturally respond to those thoughts and emotions. Although I was whole, it was a surprise to see the effect of this stressful time years later. God doesn't just want our soul and spirit to be healed, but our physical body as well. He has not only dealt with the sin issues of our lives, but also has made provision for the ramifications of sin on our bodies.

My physical body responded to the stress of the affair, and over time it lowered my immune system's ability to fight. As a result, I broke out in huge amounts of skin cancer, more than the doctor had ever seen. He treated and healed it with a cream that boosted my immune system. After receiving a clean bill of health, I asked him, "Is the sun still my enemy?" He responded, "The sun never *was* your enemy. Some people have this type of skin cancer on the bottoms of their feet!"

Peace in the heart is the biggest immune booster of all. The cancer was a physical manifestation of an inward problem I was dealing with. The doctor said, "You've really had a battle here, haven't you?" "Yes," I replied, holding back the tears, "we have."

Another physical ailment that was beginning to bother me was pain on my right side, right below the ribs. The pain had increased to the point where I felt I would need to see a doctor. Dr. Don, who *is* a medical doctor, identified my gall bladder as the source of the pain. He said that this was a sign of unforgiveness. I felt like saying, "Tell me something I *don't* know!"

Resentment and bitterness are deadly emotions, and I found out that they were definitely the cause of the pain in my gallbladder. I know this because that night as we prayed together, I felt a warm spot under my ribs. The pain was gone instantly. I was healed as the unforgiveness lifted from me. I haven't had a problem with it since, except when I get anxious, angry, or upset! It is my little gauge to help me keep myself pure in thought and forgiveness!

The Lord longs to heal people and make them whole. So many who suffer through adultery in their marriage are still not "over it" ten, fifteen, twenty, or twenty-five years later. Too many only survive through it and miss the pleasure of thriving in relationships again. Not long ago, an older man pulled me into a back hall after hearing Audrey and me speak. His wife had passed away years before. He told me, "I had an affair years ago and never told my wife." He had confided in a pastor. That pastor had told the man's wife on her deathbed and his whole family found out. He had been alienated from his own children and family ever since. Then he looked at me, and I will never forget what he said: "You are a blessed man that your wife loved you enough to tell you. How I wish *I* had confessed."

We meet so many people who regret their involvement with adultery, and we also find that people walk this road blindly, not knowing that there are steps leading to it that aren't obvious at all. There are unnoticed and inappropriate relationships that are seemingly innocent, when a man and a woman are "just friends." What most people are unaware of is an epidemic, which we'll call "soulical" adultery. This is the emotional attachment that takes place before physical adultery, and it's extremely entrapping.

King David's affair with Bathsheba is perhaps one of the most talked about in the Bible. We are living in a time where we should be preparing for battle. There is serious war against the family in our divorce culture. David sent the armies off to war, while he stayed home. While relaxing (being lazy), David saw Bathsheba and noticed that she was very beautiful. He inquired. He lay with her. She returned to her house. The next thing David heard was the news that changed everything: "I'm pregnant."

How well I remember that moment. At the time, it "felt" like a harsh form of discipline. Of course, feelings are real, but they're not true. All of a sudden, it seemed as though "normal" life as I knew it was about to end. At the same time, strangely enough, it seemed completely and plainly unbelievable. My whole world stopped for a moment at the news.

David became an adulterer and a murderer without intention. In a similar way, sexual sin was released into my life without my realizing how it happened. I think the same thing happened with David, and it happens regularly among people and leaders in the body of Christ.

Sure, there are those who simply choose to walk that road. It's premeditated and isn't a trap at all. It is blatant and is intended as an escape and, sometimes, as vengeance. Surprisingly, however, this is the minority.

*Infidelity doesn't come out of nowhere. It is the result of a process.*

For most people who get "caught" in a predicament, it crept up on them. They didn't realize that those small and seemingly innocent compromises were about to lead to that sin that everybody hates to talk about: adultery. How does this happen? First of all, in David's case, he didn't discern the season. He should have been fighting the battle, but he was taking a nap. After his nap he went to the roof, where his eyes saw something he wanted. He took a long gaze.

But it was more than this. There was something in David's heart that released this to happen. Infidelity doesn't come out of nowhere. It is the result of a process; the same process that leads unwary church leaders into sexual sin. Farmers use the same process when planting a field. It's called the law of sowing and reaping.

Everybody knows that if a farmer plants corn seed, corn will grow—every time, without fail. It's not as though the farmer sees it come up and thinks, *"Surprise, surprise! How did that get there? Did it just pop up out of nowhere?"* Of course not.

In the same way, there is a process of sowing and reaping that causes people to "fall" in love. Our dear friend, Craig Hill, of Family Foundations International, is the one who introduced us to the term *"soulical" adultery.* He describes falling in love like a bank account. One can make deposits and withdrawals from this bank, and credit is determined. This approach certainly demystifies the whole idea of "falling in love!"

I opened up my heart in a friendship and shared funny moments and interesting conversation. This may sound innocent and normal in every way, and it was—at first. I was accepted and received, and a deposit was made. Credit occurred. This happened between both of us over and over again; we were sowing and reaping into each other's hearts. This experience made both of us feel super-fantastic! A "feeling" of love grew in my heart. I found myself wanting to be with that person. It's an emotional "feel good" experience! What I didn't know was that this relationship became soulical adultery. It was just a matter of time before it turned physical.

The opposite began to take place as well. I may have wanted to reach out to Bob for interesting conversation and fun moments and felt shut down. Rejected. Now there's a negative balance. It wasn't anything Bob did or even said. I may simply have been expecting too much and felt disappointed. Nonetheless, this made it naturally more difficult for me to open up the next time. I gravitated to the one who was feeding my cravings with mounds of attention. Eventually, walls went up around my heart to protect myself from hurt, and the honest communication between me and Bob dissolved.

It's a setup. We all need an outlet to communicate the deep issues of our heart. If we aren't communicating with our spouse, we will communicate with someone else. Whenever we share more deeply with someone other than our spouse—whether male or female—even to the point of sharing news *first* with this other person, we have entered the arena of soulical adultery. It is the first step towards sexual adultery. It means we are bonding and uniting with that person, giving to that person what belongs only in covenant. When we do that, what happens? We credit their love bank, which will cause their heart to "fall in love" with us.

I had a problem with hardness of heart. I was full of pride, and in order to make things go my way, I always made sure I was in control. I decided not to let Bob in. I didn't know it at the time, but my actions confirmed it. The Bible identifies those with hardness of heart as those who trust in the flesh (themselves), instead of the Lord. When a person has a hardened heart it can be very destructive to a marriage.

There's a battle between the flesh and the spirit with the soul as the prize! A person trusting in himself is seeking to preserve his own life. Instead of trusting in the Lord Jesus, he utilizes his own defense mechanisms and tactics to keep himself from being hurt. What he doesn't realize is that he has a hardened heart.

Surprisingly, hard-hearted people often appear outwardly to be anything but hard-hearted. Many times they are outgoing, bold, gifted, anointed, and usually very service-oriented. Although these characteristics are not automatic symptoms of hard-heartedness, they are common. Many service-oriented people such as pastors, doctors, and counselors tend to become hard-hearted because their professions are such that they open their hearts to others, thus making themselves vulnerable. Call it an "occupational hazard." More often than not, this hardness of heart is hidden from every-one, including themselves! That's how it was with me.

Service-oriented people always face potential rejection. As the old saying goes, "You can't please all the people all the time." Others will get irritated with them and accuse them of failing to meet their expectations. Repeated hurt and rejection of this nature can cause service-oriented peo-ple to develop a hardened heart for protection against future hurt and rejection. They put up a wall.

I can relate to this beginning as a very young child. Even though my home was exceptionally loving and peaceful, I strived to keep it that way. I decided from the beginning of my life to make everyone around me happy—at any cost. If I ever had an angry or negative thought, I just stuffed it. This behavior taught me to be in control; self-dependent.

How does the devil destroy families? Often, he sets up young children to have hardened hearts, unable to share who they are. Deep down, the core fear of my life is fear of failure, of failing to make everyone happy. During the time of the affair, Bob was not a very happy person. I embraced this as personal failure. On the flipside, I had a great ability to make this other person happy! That was my setup for destruction.

My hard heart found an outlet. The flow of life emotional-ly began to spill over, and I felt great when I was around him. I remember when Bob took me out for lunch one day and confronted me about this relationship. I firmly objected, insisting that there was nothing romantic going on! Little did I know that it was just a matter of time. The law of sowing and reaping was in effect. Something was growing between us.

When I began to have romantic feelings, I felt guilty about it, but pushed it aside and didn't share it with anyone. The enemy had me isolated. One day, opportunity presented itself and I compromised a little, and then a little more the next time. The next thing I knew, it was sexual.

In my case with Bob, I never got to the point where I wanted to leave my marriage. I never doubted my love with Bob, and I never replaced what Bob and I had with this other relationship. But I was definitely shocked, afraid, and wounded. I wished I felt more guilty, because I knew I should. I felt remorse, but not repentance. This truly revealed my hardened heart.

What does God do? What happens when sin increases? Grace abounds. God's kindness is meant to lead us to repentance. God's goodness and kindness were poured out to me. I know that is how I came to the point of repentance. For me, it was just a matter of weeks. I wanted to end the relationship and tell Bob. I wanted to deal with all of it.

I am so thankful for our time in Phoenix. I submitted myself to Bob and to our godly counselors to the point where I would do anything they said. I had to relinquish control. Interestingly enough, that continues to be the case. I never want to have that love for control again. Because I see myself as "nice" and "sweet," the deception of lust for control can be very subtle. I beg the Lord to keep me safe from my own self.

One of the last things we have done to protect our marriage is to make sure we have breaks from intense ministry. Our friendship is deep, our laughter together is explosive, and our communication is blatantly honest. There are many things that led me to the place of adultery. I was burned out. I was way too busy and bored at the same time. I wasn't connecting on a real deep level with Bob or anyone else, because I had trained myself to keep from saying anything negative. What I didn't know was that this was the fruit of a hardened heart. I wanted control. I wanted to be the martyr. But when I started making deposits in another person's love bank, and he deposited back to me, a very deadly fruit arose. My heart was revealed for what it was.

*There is only one way to choose life and be acceptable to God...the finished work of Jesus Christ within us.*

I am so thankful that Bob has forgiven me for the sin I committed against him. When we made covenant on our marriage day, I said that I would give myself to him. My body was no longer my own. When I selfishly gave some-thing away that was not mine to give, I stole from him. I am thankful for the healing balm of the Lord Jesus to forgive, restore, and bring us into a relationship in which we com-municate deeply.

Oh, the blessings for those who trust in the Lord, for those who don't trust in their own ambitions and talents! One of my favorite songs to play on the piano and sing is a song entitled, "You Are My Hiding Place."

I consciously ask the Lord to humble me daily. I found out that my heart is deceitful and full of pride. But I also discovered that the Lord Himself would rescue me, help me, and protect me from my own wickedness. In fact, as I hide myself in Him, He *is* my righteousness. It's not something I strive for; I simply rest in it. I don't attain to it—I hide in it. *As long as your soul is alive unto itself, it's inviting death. There is only one way to choose life and be acceptable to God...the finished work of Jesus Christ within us.*

⊹══ ══⊹

The day came when our natural love and affection ran out. That's when we had to learn what true love was really all about. It wasn't about roles or expectations or being a "good" husband or a "good" wife or raising a "good" family or just getting along together; all of those are possible in the natural. It was when we faced a crisis that nearly tore us apart that we learned that we needed a love that was beyond ourselves, a supernatural love, a love that finds both its source and its fulfillment in God, a love that is eternal and can face any threat and overcome any obstacle.

The journey of learning supernatural love lasts a lifetime. The Lord taught me that He was the God of rest, not forced feelings. Natural and logical love is self-serving and self-protecting. Supernatural love always gives without expectation. Sometimes I cry when I think about Bob. I love him without restraint. Our God of restoration and unconditional love has brought our marriage to a place of rest and safety. The laughter between us flows easily, and new hope for the future allows us to dream again.

Out of our tenacious desperation, we found *dependence*.

# *Released*

Upon our return to Winnipeg, we re-entered a life very similar to the one that we had left two years before when we moved to Phoenix. There were, however, some significant differences. First of all, *we* were different; me, Bob, our kids—all of us. No one who goes through what we went through comes out unchanged. Bob often says, "Change is inevitable, but growth is optional." The past two years had brought enormous changes in our lives and circumstances; the question was, had we grown?

Without a doubt. We understood ourselves—our weaknesses as well as our strengths—better than we ever had before. We learned that our own natural love for each other was not enough to sustain us when the greatest trial of all came along. We knew the absolute sufficiency of the grace of God as well as the abundant extravagance of His love.

The biggest change of all, of course, or at least the most obvious, was Robert. Bob and I went to Phoenix with three children and came back with four. From the very beginning, Robert had stolen the hearts of every other member of the Meisner clan. Our three children adored him. And it made my heart rejoice to see the way Bob had taken to him. He was always tickling Robert or wrestling with him or loving on him in some way. Bob admits that he struggled with his fears about the baby right up until his birth. "Then," he says, "everything changed completely. As soon as Robert was born, I said, 'That's *my* boy. He is *my* son.'" Ever since, Bob has been Robert's protector...and his biggest fan.

*We learned that our own natural love for each other was not enough to sustain us when the greatest trial of all came along.*

It was these changes that made moving back such a challenge. Coming home to Winnipeg forced us to come face to face with our fears and memories and the inevitable revelation of our "big secret." As we soon learned, this too was part of God's restoration plan, a part we might have chosen to avoid had we not committed ourselves to humble and trusting obedience to His will. As painful as it might be, we knew that the Lord wanted us to go full circle. It was time to deal with every skeleton in our closet and face the adversity that would surely come against us.

Rumors were flying everywhere about our marriage. Most people had figured out what had happened and were

154

criticizing us for running away and not "fessing up." From our perspective, we were in a time of rescue, and God kept us hidden and protected until we healed up. Either way, we were extremely thankful for the time we had away from Winnipeg. The shock was over, our sweet baby boy had been born, and we had learned that we could depend on God daily for whatever came our way.

Once back in Winnipeg, Bob and I rejoined the staff of *It's A New Day*. We recognized even then that we would need to "go public" with our story, and probably sooner rather than later. Aside from a couple of very close friends that I had confided in, no one in Winnipeg outside of our family knew any details. Rumor and speculation abounded. My dad had even begun to receive anonymous phone calls insisting that something fishy was going on and threatening to bait the media to get at the truth.

It was important for us to tell our story soon in order to avoid a scandal. Besides, it was the right thing to do. It would be much better for everyone to hear it from us rather than through the media, because then there would be nothing hidden for the media to "discover" and turn into a huge negative exposé. We also hoped that telling our story would bring encouragement to many who heard it.

We were certainly mindful of the scandals of recent years when high-profile Christian leaders had "fallen from grace" as a result of media revelations of moral or financial failures. Such public exposure of their sins cast shame and dishonor on the name of Jesus and inflicted great damage on the body of Christ. This we were determined to avoid at all costs.

These earlier incidents had become scandals because those involved did not repent and confess and "come clean" on their own but were exposed. They were "found out," which created a strong perception in the mind of the public that they had tried to cover up their activities.

In our situation, we *wanted* to come out. We wanted to be open and honest about what had happened not only because we were public figures, but also because it was part of our restoration process. My "private" sin had some very public ramifications, and it was important to be up front about it, particularly for those people who knew us or knew of us or knew our ministry and who would stand to be hurt the most by knowledge of what had happened. Our desire was to handle the whole matter with honesty, transparency, and integrity.

With all of these factors in mind, we set a date for a television appearance on *It's A New Day*. As much as I wanted to do this and as much as I knew it needed to be done, I have to admit it was really tough. A few of our very closest friends came to the studio to bring support through intense prayer. I prayed that I wouldn't cry but instead communicate strength in God and hope for marriages. It was a very sober moment. Now the world would officially know the absolute worst thing I had ever done.

Dad interviewed us, which gave us the opportunity to thank him and Mom publicly for their unconditional love and covering through it all. I had no idea that Bob was going to do this, but as we began talking, he took off his jacket and placed it on my shoulders as an act of "covering." I knew I was protected and loved but at the same time, part of me felt exposed and ashamed.

The program managed to shock many people. Viewer response was quite high, most of it thanking us for our courage and voicing support for our marriage. Some, however, responded with judgment and criticism, and tried to place shame on me.

No one had to tell me anything about shame. I had lived with it intimately for the last two years. Only through the journey of radical repentance that God led me on was I released from shame. Shame isn't something God invented; it's the residue of sin. Once forgiveness comes, shame is taken away.

*Shame isn't something God invented; it's the residue of sin. Once forgiveness comes, shame is taken away.*

That doesn't mean I had no more struggles with shame. After we returned to Winnipeg and I began working at my parents' ministry again, I could feel it in the air. Countless times I sat in my car and prayed to God and listened to get His perspective. I needed to be reminded about how He felt about me. I always entered the building with a smile and a hello, but it was hard to dodge the fiery spears of judgment and the accusing and condemning looks people would give me out of the corner of their eye. I felt as though I was on probation; that I was being watched to see when it would happen again or whether I was truly sorry for what I did.

Essentially, it's a trust issue. In Phoenix, we were actively involved in ministry even as we were being healed. Nobody there, either inside or outside the church, gave us any problem. It was different in Winnipeg. There were staff members who felt I was disqualified for ministry and didn't deserve to come back. They questioned my motives, and some even questioned the nature of my parents' relationship with God because they had allowed me to come back. Others were jealous at the thought that Bob and I could be healed and happy together. Their attitude was, "Audrey doesn't deserve that. She has no right to be that happy."

It really hurts when people who call themselves friends consider you permanently disqualified for ministry because of one transgression. This is not to diminish in any way the magnitude of my sin; it was huge! It's just that when we repent, God forgives, and when He forgives, He also restores. Restoration is another word for *redemption*, and God is always in the redemption business.

One lesson I have learned in dealing with the criticism is that my sole responsibility in it all is my *response*. It's that simple. I'm not responsible to defend myself or to prove myself to be right. I *am* responsible to live my life in humble surrender and obedience to the Lord who forgave me, healed me, and restored me. Opportunities for forgiveness continue for a lifetime, and we have a lifetime to forgive as Jesus did. In the end, His assessment of my life and faithfulness is all that matters.

In the early days of our rescue, right after this whole business started, there were people "in the know" who were concerned about what this would do to Mom and Dad's ministry. Some even advised them to write us off because we were tainted and damaged goods and the ministry was too important. The bottom line is that they did not believe we *could* be restored without damaging the ministry. Their underlying perspective was that there was no hope. They assumed that our marriage could never be strong again and that we could never be useful or effective in ministry.

Bob and I are so thankful for the attitude that my mom and dad took. For them, the choice was easy: family comes first. Family trumps everything else. There is a mentality among some in Christian ministry that *nothing* is more important than the ministry organization. They forget that the family was the first institution that God set in place, centuries before there was even a church, much less ministry organizations to support the church. At one point, my parents told us, "Even if we lose the ministry over this, our biggest concern is for you and your family. If we lose everything when this comes out, so be it, as long as you don't lose each other."

*The family was the first institution that God set in place, centuries before there was even a church. Family trumps everything else.*

Now, two years later, the ministry was still there and still thriving, but survival did not come without a cost. A number of the staff left, saying that they could no longer respect my parents as leaders.

One staff member said, "It's too soon for them to come back." When asked to specify what length of time was sufficient, he had no answer. Was it because we were not properly accountable? Was it because we took the whole thing too lightly? Was it because we had not shown fruits of genuine repentance? He had no solid basis for his judgment. So often, people's judgment is not based on biblical teaching, but on feelings of superiority or jealousy, or on some control issue.

Sometimes it is simply a lack of faith. They simply cannot believe that full restoration can occur in a marriage rocked by adultery. This is because they have rarely, if ever, seen it happen. Much of the western Christian world has unwittingly bought into secular "pop" psychology with its "anything goes" philosophy and its attitude that no relationships are necessarily permanent, not even marriage. It is just such a mind-set, which has lost all concept of covenant, that feeds our contemporary divorce culture. Even in the church, divorce is often the commonly accepted remedy for adultery. For some reason, we believe that God can forgive, but He cannot restore.

That's *not* the God of the Bible! God *does* forgive *and* restore. He redeems and He heals even the most broken of people and releases them to fruitful ministry again. Bob and I are living proof. Since the original broadcast in which Bob and I told our story, countless viewers have related to us how encouraged they have been to see not just people in a TV ministry, but real people who are working through real issues; people who have been through hell on earth and not only survived, but are flourishing.

One of the things that Bob and I love doing together is decorating and designing. We relish the creative challenge of transforming the appearance of a room according to the design we conceive in our minds. Often, as we work together, we listen to teaching tapes. One night, while installing a "faux floor," we were listening to our dear friend, Dr. Jim Richards, on the subject of "defining moments."

Jim explained that people love to define us by the worst thing we've done...by the mistakes in our lives. It is human nature to remember the dirt on someone rather than to build them up by playing up their accomplishments. But that is completely contrary to God's way. When God forgives us, He forgets what we've done. He takes these broken pots of clay (us!) and molds us and beautifies us into extravagant vessels to hold His glory. The choice is ours how we will define our lives. We can take our times of hardship and let God get deep in the molding process, or we can live with the fact that we're just sinners. (By the way, so is everyone else!) That night, I again let God minister acceptance and love to me. He still had dreams and desires to use me, and I could let myself get discouraged by what others thought, or I could define my life by His grace.

I refuse to be defined by what people say or think about me. I would much rather be defined by who God says I am. Sometimes in this context I think of Mary Magdalene. Although she is widely known as an adulterous woman—the judgment of man—the Bible also talks about her extravagant worship and generous giving, which I am sure is how God defined her. Now that I have shared with everybody the absolute worst thing I've ever done, there's not much left, yet I am so defined by my God that it doesn't matter what people say.

People have said (and will continue to say) that I am disqualified; they may judge and criticize me, but that's not my responsibility. My response is my responsibility. If I respond out of selfishness, I could easily get into my own judgment problem. If I let the Lord define me, however, then it is easy for me to live free because I know who I am. I am not an adulterous woman. My Lord tells me that I am clothed in white robes of righteousness and purity.

Soon after our return to Winnipeg, Bob and I began hosting *It's A New Day* with my mom and dad, and that took us into leaps and bounds of healing. It was as though each guest was speaking directly to us, and the time has been rich in teaching and ministry. We are so thankful for the opportunity to re-establish ourselves in the television ministry. More importantly, we are glad that God is getting glory for His goodness. Our journey continues, and we are beginning to face our future from a place of strength on a firm foundation; not our strength, but His and not our foundation but that which is laid in the amazing grace, abundant mercy, and extravagant love of our Lord Jesus Christ.

Audrey and I are on a journey that continues to take us from glory to glory. In the pages of this book, we have attempted to describe that journey as openly and as honestly and as transparently as we can because we believe that everything that happens in our lives has a purpose. This does *not* mean that it was God's purpose for adultery to invade our marriage and nearly destroy our relationship. God's purpose *never* includes sin. The terrorist attack that ambushed our marriage was Satan's attempt to destroy our lives and break apart something that God had brought together. The testimony of our journey is that God took the ugliest, worst, and most horrible thing that had ever happened to us—adultery and an unexpected pregnancy—and turned it to His purpose. He brought beauty out of ashes, rejoicing out of sorrow, and laughter out of weeping. Most of all, He took that which the enemy sowed into our lives with malicious intent and turned it into the most precious gift we could ever imagine—our son Robert.

*God took the ugliest, worst, and most horrible thing that had ever happened to us and turned it to His purpose.*

Like the Good Shepherd that He is, the Lord led us safely through the valley of the shadow of death—through heartache and pain, anguish and sorrow, anger and bitterness, and rejection and shame—back into the Promised Land of love and light, mercy and grace, and forgiveness and redemption. He took us from the barren wilderness of doubt and devastation into the fertile valleys of confident assurance and humble dependence upon Him. Along the way He opened up to us new dimensions of His nature and character that have put us in awe of the greatness and majesty of our God as never before. He mended our shattered hopes and restored our broken dreams so that today, against all human logic and expectations to the contrary, Audrey and I enjoy a marriage that is stronger, better, and more vibrant with love and life than it has ever been. It has nothing to do with us, but everything to do with Him.

This is our journey and our story. Everybody has a story, and everyone is on a journey. Your story may be similar to ours or it may be completely different; what we have in common is the journey. Like the children of Israel, as children of God we are all on a journey from the wilderness to the Promised Land.

We can look at marriage the same way. As Christian couples we must navigate our way through the barren wilderness of our contemporary divorce culture, a culture characterized by confusion, cynicism, relativism, and false conceptions of love and intimacy—a culture of *quiet desperation*—into the Promised Land of growth, fruitfulness, and release into the full purposes of God.

God has a "Promised Land marriage" for every couple willing to pay the price.

When the Israelites came out of Egypt, they left behind a life of slavery and bondage. God's intention was to take them into the land of Canaan, the Promised Land, right away. Because of their disobedience and lack of faith, however, they wandered in the wilderness for forty years. They were too attached to the memories of their past in Egypt to press forward into their future in God's purpose. Symbolically, the story of the exodus is the story of the journey from sin to righteousness; from slavery to Satan's deception into freedom as God's children. Before the Israelites could leave the wilderness, they had to leave the sin they loved. They had to make the deliberate choice to leave the past behind and move forward. They had to change their desires.

No one can enter the Promised Land by staying where they are. We must be willing to leave our past, surrender up the sin we love, and change our desire to seek the fullness of God rather than settle for the barrenness of the worldly culture in which we live.

After Moses died, Joshua led the Israelites across the Jordan River into the land of Canaan. According to the Bible, the Jordan was in its annual flood season: high, rushing water with lots of debris. It seems amazing that God chose that season for them to cross, yet He wanted them to know beyond a doubt that it was by His power and not their own that they accomplished it. The Israelites had to respond in faith. As soon as the priests who were carrying the ark of the covenant set foot in the water, the waters of the river parted and rolled back all the way to a place called Adam. The curse on man was broken all the way back to Adam, the first man.

The Jordan River was a formidable obstacle that the Israelites had to overcome in moving from the wilderness to the Promised Land. From the human perspective it was daunting, fraught with peril, and seemed well nigh impossible. However, when they placed their faith in God and stepped out in obedience they discovered that the obstacle which so intimidated them was nothing to God.

In the same way, we face all sorts of obstacles in life. Marriage alone brings plenty of challenges on its own. Sometimes, especially when we are facing the greatest obstacle of our life or our marriage, we wonder why it has to be so hard. Part of the answer is because we have an enemy who hates God and wants to ruin the lives of His children. At the same time, God often uses our obstacles to draw us to Him by allowing us to see that we are inadequate to handle them alone. That's what Audrey and I discovered about our own marriage. No matter how much we loved each other or how strong we thought we were, when the greatest crisis of all came crashing down on us, we discovered that our resources were quickly depleted and totally insufficient for dealing with it. By the mercy of God, we learned through experience that *His grace is sufficient*. It was only by casting ourselves on the supernatural love of God in total dependence on Him that we found love that was sufficient to overcome the devastation of adultery.

*God often uses our obstacles to draw us to Him by allowing us to see that we are inadequate to handle them alone.*

During the most difficult season of our lives, we stepped into the river and God rolled the waters back. Now we're on the other side, beckoning others to come along. You can make it! There is hope! We have tasted and seen that the Lord is good! His mercies endure forever. Great is His faithfulness!

Many married couples today are trapped in the wilderness of a marriage where love has failed them and are sorely tempted to "return to Egypt," to bail out instead of pressing on to find God's healing grace and mercy. Others may even have been rescued from the sin they loved, yet continue to wander in disobedience, unwilling to surrender their own will. They are floundering, uncertain of what to do.

Perhaps this describes your situation. Whatever has happened in your marriage, no matter how ugly or painful, you can still have a "Promised Land marriage" if you both are willing to pay the price. Redemption never comes without a price. If you want to redeem your marriage, it will cost you: your pride, your self-righteousness, your self-reliance, your dreams (in exchange for God's dreams for you), your insistence on standing up for your own rights; something.

Mine and Audrey's redemption did not come without a price. First of all, God sent His own Son to die so that we might live and have eternal life. Our redemption cost God everything!

Second, when I found myself in this situation, I knew it was going to cost me something. If I wanted my marriage to survive, I had to be willing to give up everything else. Basically, I had two choices. I could have chosen to follow my own pride and self-righteousness and told Audrey, "I'm out of here! You made your bed, now sleep in it. You caused this mess, now you clean it up." That choice would only have fed the desperate divorce culture we live in. My other choice was to stay and fight: fight for my marriage, fight for my children, fight for the love of my wife and for the dreams we had shared together. Thanks to the help and counsel of godly people, I made the second choice.

Third, our redemption cost others something. It cost the investment of time by people like Leo and Molly Godzich, Lois Burkett, Tommy Barnett, Dr. Don and Mary Colbert, and others who counseled us, reached out to us, loved us when we couldn't love ourselves or each other. It cost Ron Hembree, who gave me a job when he didn't really need me, giving me daily strength and confidence that everything would be all right. He was in a position to help, and he helped. It cost Audrey's parents their reputation in the eyes of some who didn't think we should be allowed to reenter ministry.

Finally, there was also a financial cost: moving from Winnipeg to Phoenix, then to Pittsburgh, and then back to Winnipeg; selling a house quickly rather than waiting for the best price, buying another and then selling it the same way, and finally buying another house. I can honestly say that this tragedy in our lives has cost us tens of thousands of dollars...and it's worth every single penny. We had to give up some things, but the joy that we experience now, and the wholeness of my family and my children and my marriage, more than make up for what we lost.

Do you want to redeem your marriage? Do you want to enter the Promised Land? Surrender your pride, your self-righteousness, and your insistence on your "rights." Acknowledge the inadequacy of your own love and resources. Step out in faith. Plunge into your "Jordan River" and watch God roll back the waters of adversity that once seemed so certain to overwhelm you. Resource the promises in the covenant that God has made with you.

A "Promised Land marriage" is also a *covered* marriage, protected from attack and sheltered from the destructive influences of secular culture by total dependence on God and bonded together by *supernatural* love. But what qualities define a covered marriage? How do you turn a struggling, endangered, or perhaps simply tired "wilderness" marriage into a "Promised Land" marriage of strength, vitality, promise, and victory? How can a Christian marriage not only survive but also *thrive* in a culture of quiet desperation?

Here are some things that Audrey and I have learned in the course of our journey.

First, pray together as a couple—*daily*. This means more than just saying a prayer at mealtimes. Also, we're not talking about a prayer *meeting* where the two of you pray together for an hour (although that too is appropriate at times)! Daily prayer together is a time where you are intimate, transparent, gaze into each other's eyes and deal with the day's events if needed. In other words, this is a prayer time when you keep your eyes *open*.

This approach to daily prayer was modeled for us by Leo and Molly, and it is one of the greatest and most valuable gifts we have ever received. Essentially, it is a very simple prayer model (and simple is usually the best kind). Begin by looking at each other face-to-face and eye-to-eye. Try to find Jesus in each other. Remember, *He* is your source, your answer, and your supreme love. As you pray, focus on three things:

*A "Promised Land marriage" is a covered marriage, protected from attack and sheltered from destructive influences by total dependence on God.*

Thankfulness. Take turns expressing what you are thankful for that day, not just in general but also what you are thankful for about each other.

Repentance. Once again, take turns asking if there is anything that either of you hurt the other with today. If so, before God and your spouse, confess it and repent of it. The only response the other should make is, "I forgive you."

Bless each other. Speak blessing and goodness to each other. This will help each of you focus on the positives about each other rather than the negatives. This is one way of living out Paul's instruction in Philippians 4:8: *"Finally, brethren, whatever things are true, whatever things are noble, whatever things are just, whatever things are pure, whatever things are lovely, whatever things are of good report, if there is any virtue and if there is anything praiseworthy—meditate on these things."*

This daily prayer time is also a great time to talk and pray about your future together and your dreams. In the midst of hard times, it is often difficult to dream, but prayer clears our vision because it shifts our focus from our problems to the Problem Solver so we can see from His perspective once more. Remember, the Lord is not only a Redeemer, but also a *re-dreamer*. Through prayer, He will help you dream again. Regular, daily prayer together will launch you as a couple into your destiny because it is in the place of prayer that you will *discover* your destiny.

Prayer is such a big part of our lives today; so much more than it used to be. The change came when we reached the end of our resources and discovered that they weren't enough. One thing about surrender and dependence is that they help you realize how much you need prayer. Audrey and I no longer take our marriage for granted. We have decided that we need the Lord in every dream and in every purpose, and everything we pray for, we pray *specifically*.

We cannot overstate the importance of making prayer together a *daily* practice. Even today, years later, whenever we see or talk to Leo, he asks, "Are you still praying together every day?" It's that important. Don't neglect it.

Another priority for a "covered" marriage is for each partner to focus on drawing closer to the Lord. James 4:8 promises, *"Draw near to God and He will draw near to you."* Too often when married couples seek to improve their marriage and increase intimacy, they direct all their attention to getting closer to each other and ignore the spiritual dimension. That's the wrong approach. The way to get closer to each other is by getting closer to God.

> *The way to get closer to each other is by getting closer to God.*

Imagine an equilateral triangle with God as the top point and you and your spouse as the two bottom points. If you focus on moving toward each other (along the horizontal line of the triangle) it may seem that you are getting closer to each other, but neither of you are getting closer to God and as your baseline narrows, the entire "triangle" of your relationship becomes increasingly less stable.

Look what happens, however, when you focus on drawing near to God. As each of you seeks to get closer to God (not *independently*, but *individually*) through prayer, Bible study, surrender, and humble obedience, etc., you each begin to rise along your respective angles of the triangle toward the top point—God. As both of you draw closer to God, you are also drawing closer to each other. Drawing closer to God means knowing Him better and becoming more like Him by taking on His attributes. The more like God you both become, the more like each other you become and the closer together you grow. Focus your hearts on Him continually, and you will find yourselves closer and more intimate with each other than you ever dreamed. This is divine geometry...and it works!

A covered marriage is one where both partners live by the biblical truth that *"it is more blessed to give than to receive"* (Acts 20:35). Giving is everything! Paul tells us in Ephesians that marriage is a picture of Christ's relationship with us, His church. The church is the bride and He is the Bridegroom who gave His life for His bride. We, in turn, give our lives to Him in faithful, humble surrender and obedience or, in other words, by dying to self. This kind of relationship is not give/take but give/give.

Marriage is the same way. There are seasons in every marriage when one spouse or the other feels that he or she is doing all the giving. This season may last days, years, or even decades. Unfortunately, many times it is true. A spouse who continually takes while the other gives sucks the life right out of a marriage.

Whole people are givers, not takers. This is why it is so important that both partners in a marriage be whole people; people who know who they are in themselves as well as in Christ and who do not need or look to their spouse to be either their source or their answer. Whole people are complete within themselves and their relationship with Christ and have no need to look to their spouse to complete them. This frees them up to give. As long as one or the other spouse is incomplete, and therefore taking rather than giving, the marriage will not be whole. When both partners are totally committed to giving to the other, both will receive everything they need.

There is a story about a woman who decided she'd had a few too many decades of "putting up with" her husband. She visited a lawyer and asked him how she could divorce her husband in such a way as to hurt him the most. The lawyer suggested that she spend the next three or four months giving extravagantly to her husband and expressing love to him in every way possible. After he was convinced that she totally loved him, she could slam the shocking divorce papers in his face.

Liking the idea, the woman went home and put the plan into effect. Things did not turn out the way she expected. The more she gave to her husband, the more he began to respond to her needs. The more she expressed her love for him, the more loving she began to feel toward him, and the more loving he became toward her. She sowed seeds of love, acceptance, and admiration, and surprisingly enough, began to reap a similar harvest in return. By the time the four months were up, all thoughts of divorce had been forgotten.

Another vital key to a covered and protected marriage is to remember that your spouse is neither your answer nor your enemy. When Audrey and I married, I thought she was my joy, my answer. In my eyes she was infallible, God's special gift to mankind, and I was lucky enough to be the man. Seventeen years later, I discovered she wasn't. How could someone so beautiful and wonderful cause so much pain?

*Remember that your spouse is neither your answer nor your enemy.*

Through much pain and prayer and yielding to God, I came to the understanding that, as wonderful and gracious and loving as Audrey is, she is not my joy or my answer, and I am not hers. And she is certainly not infallible, and neither am I. None of us are. Our only answer is Christ and our only joy is in Him alone. As Audrey and I learn more and more how to see Christ in each other, we experience more and more joy in each other's company, because we are feeling His joy through each other. It is only when we lose ourselves in Christ that we truly find ourselves; and when we find ourselves in our identity with Christ, that is when His joy becomes full in us and we realize that He is our source and no one else.

Marriages always run into trouble when one spouse looks to the other as his or her answer. I don't want Audrey to see me as her answer; I want her to see Jesus as her answer. I want to stay close and intimate with Jesus not only for my own spiritual health, but also in order that Audrey may not have me alone, but have Jesus through me. That's what love is. I want to be a conduit, a pipeline through which the love and grace and mercy of the Lord can flow to touch my family and everyone around me. It is in Him that I live and move and have my being. This requires dying to myself, seeking to reach the place where Paul was when he said, *"I have been crucified with Christ; it is no longer I who live, but Christ lives in me; and the life which I now live in the flesh I live by faith in the Son of God, who loved me and gave Himself for me"* (Galatians 2:20). I don't want to be Audrey's answer; I want her to be in touch with *the* Answer. I want her to look to Jesus, the author and finisher of her faith.

Just as your spouse is not your answer, he or she is also not your enemy. So often when problems arise in a marriage, spouses end up pitting themselves against each other as adversaries rather than coming together to work things out. It is this attitude that fills the divorce courts of the land.

In classical warfare strategy, a general can gain a significant advantage if he can get his opponents to see each other as enemies rather than allies and start fighting between themselves. This strategy is called "divide and conquer," and Satan has been using it effectively for ages. If he can get spouses to see each other as the enemy, he has already won ninety percent of the battle.

Don't view your spouse as your enemy, but as your ally, and even more, as being one flesh with you. You are both walking the same road; you are both on the same journey.

Maybe your situation is different. Maybe your marriage has already broken up or is on the verge of it and the prospects of restoring it are slim. You may feel that there is no "happily ever after" for your marriage. God's restoration is available for anyone who wants it and is willing to pay the price, but it will take both of you. If your spouse or ex-spouse is unwilling, there is little you can do other than pray.

*God can redeem even your very worst mistakes. Forgiveness is available for the asking.*

But that "little" is a lot! Nothing is impossible with God, and if you pray faithfully, you never can tell what might happen. God can turn around even the most impossible-seeming situations.

Even if He doesn't, don't give up. *You* can still be restored even if your marriage is not. You still have the opportunity to live in wholeness once again. Remember that your spouse or ex-spouse is not your answer or your enemy. Focus on hearing God's voice and growing in intimacy with Him. He is always your place of rest and safety.

Search your heart and ask God to reveal what is there. Are you harboring unforgiveness? Bitterness? Anger? Hatred? Surrender these to God and allow Him to release you from them and see your life transformed. God's love for you is extravagant and it is eternal. His plan for you is irrevocable. He can redeem even your very worst mistakes. Forgiveness is available for the asking. Let the Lord take your place of brokenness and make it whole and new again. Let Him bring you beauty for your ashes. No matter what has happened in your past, you are precious in His sight and He still has a bright future and a glorious destiny for you...if you let Him. Open your heart, surrender to Him, and let Him rescue you, restore you, and release you!

One day while Audrey and I were still in the midst of our drama, someone said to me "Someday, you're going to thank God for this!" At that time, those were fighting words for me! How could I ever thank God for devastation and pain? How could I ever thank Him for an ugly rubbish ash heap? I soon came to learn that God and God alone could take my ashes and my sin and my bitterness and exchange them for something beautiful. I saw that for sure the day Robert was born.

Today I can say without hesitation that the greatest love gift that God has ever given me is my son Robert. In His love, God was able to see way beyond me and say, "Bob, this child will forever be a trophy of My grace." Too often we allow ourselves to be defined by our failures when instead we are truly defined by God's intervention, and His mercy and grace extended to our lives. God knew that if He had not given us this child, we probably would have stuffed our feelings, our brokenness, our confusion, our hurt and anger inside and never dealt with them. I would have remained enraged and embittered, and very possibly ended up divorced. That would have been a disaster and a major victory for the enemy. Instead, during the nine months of Audrey's pregnancy, I let it all hang out. I left no stone unturned. God began to remove those "uglies" and replace them with Himself. I had to go to Him for everything. In the process, I learned that we *have* to get alone with God. He *has* to be our source. What does He give us? Jesus. And Jesus is all we need.

God can do infinitely more than we could ever dream or imagine or hope for.[1] He causes all things to work together for good to those who love God and are called according to His purpose.[2] When God restores us, He brings us back to our

*Cover your marriage and protect your family by casting yourself into the arms of a God who loves you.*

original design and intent in His plan. The enemy sowed death and destruction in our lives, but God transformed them into life and redemption. If He did it for us, He can do it for anybody. No matter who you are or what your circumstances may be, the God who is Love can take your defeats and turn them into victories, your failures into successes, your mourning into laughter, and your sorrow into joy. If you will let Him, He can and will restore your marriage or whatever else is broken in your life, because He is a God of amazing, awesome, and extravagant love.

In fact, God can restore us to better than we were before, to a higher purpose and intent. C. S. Lewis, in his book, *Miracles*, put it this way:

> For God is not merely mending, not simply restoring a status quo. Redeemed humanity is to be something more glorious than unfallen humanity would have been...The greater the sin, the greater the mercy: the deeper the death, the brighter the rebirth.[3]

Although Lewis was speaking of redeemed humanity as a whole, his words apply equally well to marriage relationships.

Don't succumb to the culture of quiet desperation; there is hope in the Lord. Don't allow your marriage to be broken by the enemy and end up on the trash heap of our divorce-ridden society. *Cover* your marriage and protect your family by casting yourself into the arms of a God who loves you with a wonderful, supernatural, extravagant love. No matter where you are now, He can raise you higher than you were. No matter how destitute you are, He can rescue you; no matter how broken, He can restore you; no matter how bound, He can release you. He is God Almighty, Maker of heaven and earth, our Redeemer and, *yes!...our Re-dreamer!*

> *The Lord has appeared of old to me, saying: "Yes, I have loved you with an everlasting love; therefore with lovingkindness I have drawn you"* (Jeremiah 31:3).

> *Fear not, for I am with you; be not dismayed, for I am your God. I will strengthen you, yes, I will help you, I will uphold you with My righteous right hand* (Isaiah 41:10).

## Endnotes

1. Ephesians 3:20, paraphrased.

2. Romans 8:28, paraphrased.

3. C. S. Lewis, *Miracles* (San Francisco: HarperSanFrancisco, a division of HarperCollins Publishers, 1947, HarperCollins ed. 2001), 198.

# Bob and Audrey Meisner

Bob and Audrey Meisner are co-hosts of the television program, *It's A New Day*, seen daily across Canada and the U.K. Individually and as a couple, they have been working in Christian television since 1984.

Having pioneered in broadcasting and church planting, Bob and Audrey are now popular marriage conference speakers. Together they are committed to communicating God's love to a hurting world. They are passionate about marriages being everything God designed them to be

The Meisners currently live in Winnipeg, Manitoba, with their three teenagers and a three-year-old.

# Personal Journal

# Personal Journal

_____

_____

_____

_____

_____

_____

_____

_____

_____

_____

_____

_____

_____

_____

_____

_____

_____

_____

_____

_____

_____

_____

_____

_____

_____

# Personal Journal

# Personal Journal

# Personal Journal

# Personal Journal

# Personal Journal

# Personal Journal

# Personal Journal

Personal Journal

# Personal Journal

# Personal Journal

_____

_____

_____

_____

_____

_____

_____

_____

_____

_____

_____

_____

_____

_____

_____

_____

_____

_____

_____

_____

_____

_____

_____

_____

_____

# Personal Journal

# Personal Journal

# Personal Journal

# Personal Journal

_____

_____

_____

_____

_____

_____

_____

_____

_____

_____

_____

_____

_____

_____

_____

_____

_____

_____

_____

_____

_____

_____

_____

_____

# Personal Journal

# Personal Journal